"There can be a bit of truth in humor
and a bit of humor in the truth."

Brenden Blake

Also by Brenden Blake

Love & Marriage

HH
Heather Hill
Copyright © 2013 - All Rights Reserved
Illustrations, Photos, and Design by B Nelson
ISBN 10:0615926762- ISBN 13:978-0615926766

THE

Unofficial and Unauthorized

WORKPLACE SURVIVAL GUIDEBOOK

Get what you deserve by going from

EMPLOYEE TO EXECUTIVE

Go from the Basement to the Boardroom
By learning the unwritten rules of corporate life.

Brenden Blake

Preface

This guidebook is written for anyone who desires to join the corporate world or is already a member and aspires for more. It guides the reader from being an employee to becoming an executive by covering everything you need to know from the basement to the boardroom. This guidebook will provide a light to guide you through a strange and complex world.

While it is written from a corporate perspective, it can also apply to almost any organization including small businesses, nonprofits, and government agencies. The terms for these organizations are used interchangeably in order to create confusion, which as a member of the corporate world, you should get used to.

In order to acclimatize you to the ways of the corporate world, this guide is written in the language of corporate jargon. If you find errors in grammar or writing style you feel obliged to point out, get over it. The corporate world is full of people who think they know what they are doing and don't like having their mistakes pointed out. So don't. Especially if they can fire you.

Accordingly, this guide has opted for the use of 'he,' 'his,' and 'him,' not in any sexist sense, but to represent both he and she, his and hers, and him and her in order to save space. Anyone who might be offended, in our opinion, is overly concerned with trifling details and would be better off with a career in academia.

Much effort has been expended to make this text scattered, predictable, and naïve in order to provide you with a practical yet humorous guidebook that contains information that you, as an employee, ought to know. As a result, many of the various subjects contained herein have been treated with not necessarily accurate, but nevertheless unvarnished practical information.

This guide has made available for you the most definitive source of its kind, we can think of, on this topic. It will be your constant companion and a source of advice, inspiration, and amusement for all, that you will find no other place. Your company may even adopt it as their training manual. In this manner, we hope to contribute to your success in the corporate world.

All this is respectfully and humbly offered to you in a satirical guidebook thinly disguised as a humorous aid which offers insight into understanding the corporate world as we know it, or not. We trust that this guide will be accepted in the same spirit as it is offered.

Employee to Executive
Table of Contents

Your Workplace

Chapter 1   How to Get a Job And Keep It   11
Chapter 2   So You Got The Job!   15
Chapter 3   Departmental Health and Welfare   19
Chapter 4   Work and Play Well With Others, or Not   25
Chapter 5   Your Office, Your New Home   33
Chapter 6   Your Gear and Personal Equipment   39
Chapter 7   Looks Do Matter   41

Your Associates

Chapter 8   Who's In Charge?   45
Chapter 9   Getting Your Boss To Like You   47
Chapter 10   Cream Rises to the Top, But So Does Scum   53
Chapter 11   Getting Your Coworkers To Do What You Want   61
Chapter 12   Temporary Help, Permanent Entertainment   67

Your Work

Chapter 13   Handling Your Equipment around The Office   71
Chapter 14   Giving Good Discourse   79
Chapter 15   I Meet, Therefore I Am   83
Chapter 16   Coffee Breaks and Time Off For Bad Behavior   87
Chapter 17   Corporate Life and Death   99

Your Activities

Chapter 18   Elevator Etiquette,
             Getting Off On The Right Floor   107
Chapter 19   Parties and Other Important Office Events   111
Chapter 20   Is There Life After Work?   115
Chapter 21   Conventions and Other
             Acts of Controlled Violence   119
Chapter 22   Sex In The Office   125

Your Advancement

Chapter 23   Sleep Your Way to The Top   129
Chapter 24   Good Executives Do It   135
Chapter 25   You Screwed Up!   145
Chapter 26   Farewell, Get Even, Then Get Out   149

CHAPTER 1
HOW TO GET A JOB AND KEEP IT

When you begin your pursuit of a job, you will feel the joy and elation that goes along with doing something new. Don't worry, these feelings will quickly pass. Soon they will be replaced by sobering realization and later with desolation and despair.

The pursuit of a job is like any other adventure, it is a risky and dangerous enterprise fraught with traps and pitfalls. History is full of reminders of the dangers of embarking on a new adventure. Many people have struck out bravely into unfamiliar waters only to be eaten by sea monsters or sail off the edge of the earth.

Your hunt for a job should begin by determining what game you want to pursue. Much effort has been expended tracking the largest and wealthiest corporations. While it may seem worthwhile trying to bag one of these kings of the corporate jungle and a good way to get taken out to expensive restaurants for lunch, there is an easier approach.

Set your sights on small game. These are the poorest and worst run corporations, nonprofit organizations, and government agencies. This prey can be harder to find due to their short lifespan and tendency to nest in inconspicuous storefronts, vacant office buildings, and other hard-to-find out-of-the-way places.

These places make good prey as they often have low expectations and will be impressed simply because you found them. In some cases, they are so desperate you should be prepared to be hired on the spot. There is a downside, however, they tend to have a short lifespan and are often swallowed up and eaten by larger companies.

Be prepared to come to work and find that everything has been repossessed or that law enforcement officials are carrying out office records. If asked, never admit to working there as you may receive a court subpoena. Simply say that you are looking for some government office. This is a safe response as there is always one nearby.

Once you have found your target you will need ammunition. Information is the ammunition of the corporate world, so you need to get dirt on your target and its key executives. Or just get a key to the building. The bigger your target, the bigger the guns you will need.

Not generally recommended ways of accomplishing this task include.
1. Phone tapping.
2. Eavesdropping.

3. Stealing classified company documents.

4. Interrogating company personnel.

5. Rummaging through trash bins.

6. Divine revelation.

Armed with this information you now need to get into their offices. You can try several time proven ways people have infiltrated companies throughout history. (In order of effectiveness.)

1. Build a wooden horse and hide inside.

2. Tunnel under the building.

3. Catapult yourself over the wall.

4. Dress up like an executive.

5. Create a diversion and sneak in.

6. Call for an interview.

Now That You're In

Now that you have obtained an appointment, be sure to arrive very early. Most people think this is to show that you are responsible, but they couldn't be more wrong. This is valuable time you need to prepare for your interview. As soon as you are inside, wander around the halls eavesdropping on conversations to get information.

You can rummage through wastebaskets, filing cabinets, and unattended offices. This is so that you can find valuable information about important company personnel. Try to find the personal file of the person you are seeing. This may be difficult, but will prove worth the extra effort. Later, during the interview you can innocently ask how their treatment is coming along or how much time they really did serve.

There may be other people waiting for an interview as well, so you could just try your darndest and hope for the best. This attitude is a good way to never get hired. You have to eliminate your competition.

When you first enter the room where everyone is waiting to be interviewed you could,

1. Introduce yourself as an executive and tell everyone the job has already been filled so they can go home.

2. Introduce yourself as the fire marshal and say that the building has been condemned as a firetrap.

3. Introduce yourself as being from the Department of Health and say that you are following up a report of a highly infectious disease outbreak.

(This is just one of the many reasons you should always have a surgeon's mask and rubber gloves in your pocket, just in case. Wearing them will make this approach more convincing.)

If you are caught lying be prepared for the consequences. They may determine that you are just the sort of ambitious get up and go person that will make it in the corporate world and hire you on the spot.

To make a good impression be sure to bring along your resume. A resume is a chronological list of your education and work experience. The purpose of a resume is to give the interviewer openings to pry into your private personal affairs.

Be sure to put each listing in the best possible light, so try these examples.
1. Instead of saying that you are currently unemployed, say that you are working freelance.
2. Instead of saying that you are loud and opinionated, say that you are a management consultant.
3. Instead of saying that you were fired for being lazy, say that you parted ways over creative differences.
4. Instead of saying that you had a cut in pay, say that you left for personal principles.
5. Instead of saying that your salary was $9,425.95, say that you made six figures last year (by counting past the decimal point).

Are you concerned that you don't have any good references? Then do what many ambitious people do, make them up. Be sure to only use businesses or institutions of higher learning that have gone out of business and no longer exist so that they cannot be checked out and proven false.

How about having personal letters of reference from famous and important people like the President of the United States? Type a letter telling what a wonderful person you are and sign it from the former President of your choice. This also works for members of Congress and celebrities. Politicians are always excellent choices because they have a propensity to lie too and are naturally out of touch.

The interview is a time honored practice full of tradition that traces its roots back to something that has come to be known as the Spanish Inquisition. The purpose of the interview is not so much to gain information, but rather to interrogate and humiliate you to see if you will make it in the corporate world.

This process reached its height when the Spanish Inquisition decided to do some interviewing about the religious beliefs of the general citizenry. They found that the attitude of the public was remarkably similar to their own. Those people that lived through the interview process, that is. Time has since demonstrated that the information the interviewee gave was what the interviewer wanted to hear.

Times have changed little in this respect. Keep in mind that no matter how much people say be yourself, do not ever be yourself. These people don't know what they are talking about and are just trying to sabotage you.

Instead of being yourself, act like the person the interviewer wants to hire. If they wanted you to be yourself, they would not interview those other people for the job, they would just hire you.

In most situations the person who hires you will not be your boss. Use this fact of corporate life to your advantage. Chances are by the time you start working, the person who hired you will have forgotten everything you said. Or they will have been fired for ineptitude most likely because they hired incompetent people.

Remember, they will not always hire the person who has the best qualifications or the person who is the smartest, but rather the one who is the least threatening to take their job or who will wash their car and pick up their kids from school.

In the interview there are several topics that are important to work into the conversation to help you get hired.
1. Your past achievements going all the way back to elementary school.
2. Your contributions to society.
3. Your league batting average.
4. Your Nobel, Pulitzer, and Olympic prizes.
5. What you can do for the interviewer.
6. Your numerous awards in firearms marksmanship.

Going in for the kill. If nothing is working and all is going badly, here are some foolproof methods you can try until one of them works.
1. Lie like crazy.
2. Play dumb.
3. Cry.
4. Physical pain. (Theirs, not yours)
5. Promises of large sums of money.
6. Promise to make them Secretary of State.

Chapter 2
So You Got The Job!

Congratulations, you got the job! (Assuming you got the job.) You are now a member of the corporate world.

Welcome to the company! So, you are a member of the corporate world. At last, you will become a corporate employee among other corporate employees living the corporate way of life. Everyone has a job in a corporation and there is a job for you too in the growing corporate bureaucracy!

As a member of the corporate world, you have joined a community of individuals that has changed history and circles the globe. There is no easy way to learn the corporate way of life. Most people say that you learn them by trial and error. They have this turned around. First you make an error and then you are put on trial.

If you do not understand how the corporate world works, you will have great difficulty and hardship in adjusting to an unfamiliar way of life. This may cause you to develop a dislike for the corporate world and drive you to seek a career in government, or worse, academia.

The origins of the modern corporation are as old as mankind itself. The history of mankind can be seen as the history of the corporation beginning with primitive man's first attempt at incorporating, the limited partnership. Many scholars have tried to pinpoint the exact beginnings of the modern corporation, as we know it, with mixed success.

Some hold that the coastal cities of 9th and 10th century France and England mark the first corporate system and consequently the Vikings represent the first corporate raiders. In raiding these coastal towns they took the most useful assets including gold, silver, and women leaving the rest behind. Other scholars disagree with this as the beginnings of the modern business structure, not for any specific reason, but because they're spoiling for a fight.

Every employee is proud of his company (maybe not every employee) and is always striving to do as much as possible for it, so the higher ups will be proud of him. Hopefully, you will be working here for years to come, building memories that will last a lifetime, or at least until retirement or an indictment.

As a corporate employee, you will make fond memories of the good old days like the time the entire office computer network went down, joining the resistance during the hostile takeover, and the fourth quarter losses that forced your close friends to be fired.

You will longingly recall tales about parents' nights, the scavenger hunts for lost files, your coworker's inappropriate Halloween costume, sitting on Santa's lap at the Christmas party (come to think of it maybe that wasn't Santa after all), and the cold winter nights when songs were sung around a roaring fire after the budget cuts.

Being a member of an office is much more than going to work every day from nine to five (except on Fridays). Your office is an incubator that develops responsible employees or calculating megalomaniacs to be let loose on the unsuspecting real world.

One of the most important features of any workplace is your company logo. Your company logo is far more than some advertising gimmick devised by an executive to increase name recognition or to boost sales. It is the symbol of your company. It stands for the past, present, and future of your company. It stands for you, your coworkers, and your way of life. Your company logo is the heart and soul of your workplace.

Your company logo is steeped in history and tradition. No doubt when you join your company the history of your logo will be imparted to you by your boss. The use of the company logo has a millennium old history dating back to the marks made on the clay pots of Mesopotamia. It inspired the trade of Imperial Rome and fueled the global exploitation of the Dutch and British East India Companies.

The company logo has followed mankind across the planet and into the heavens. Ever since primitive man formed the first forerunner of the corporation, the limited partnership, the company logo has been the rallying point for corporate employees the world over.

Every week all the departments in your company will line up for the company logo ceremony. You will feel the thrill of standing at attention together with all your fellow coworkers. Your company logo, likely displayed on a flag, will enter the room accompanied by an honor guard as you wait with eager anticipation.

The command, "Salute!" is given and you salute as your company logo passes by you. As you gaze upon your company logo, you feel the thrill of being a member of your department and a part of the worldwide fellowship of corporate employees.

Then, if you are lucky, you and all your fellow corporate employees may recite The Official Corporate Pledge together. In order to ensure a properly functioning workplace the following pledge is (almost) universally adopted throughout the corporate world.

The Official Corporate Pledge

I as a member of the corporate community, I do solemnly swear that I shall,
Support the corporate way of life and all it stands for.

Keep myself neat, clean, and fully clothed in the office,
And not get caught conducting myself in any way that would bring
Disgrace or dishonor to my uniform.

Keep my desk and area in a neat and orderly fashion,
Avoiding any messy or time consuming work.
Look as if I am actually working on something, at all times.

Not borrow, steal, convert, or otherwise appropriate personal property
From my coworkers or my company,
Unless I am sure they are no longer using it, or I know they won't miss it.

Not participate in any actions that would be rude, obnoxious, or
Discourteous to my fellow coworkers,
Or cause damage to corporate offices or equipment,
Unless it's really, really funny.

Plead the fifth whenever possible,
Denying any and all responsibility for my actions.

Not leave any fires untended or feed the temporary help.

Work and play well with others, but
Not let their expectations improve the quality or quantity of my work.

Always politely and quietly listen to my boss's advice, guidance, and suggestions,
Then do what I damn well please.

And always remain loyal to my company until death do us part.
(Barring bankruptcy, firing, corporate takeover, retirement, or
Being offered a higher salary by someone else.)

Chapter 3
Departmental Health and Welfare

By now you may be asking yourself, where do I fit in?

In most jobs you will belong not only to an organization, like a corporation, company, or agency, but to a department. As important as your department is, it is not the only one in your company. Many departments combine to make up a corporation. These departments all work together, usually.

The word department is the official term for a small clique of employees. All (maybe not all) corporations are made up of a lot of these 'cliques,' or departments.

Not since high school will which clique you belong to mean so much to the quality of your life. Most of your corporate activities take place in these cliques or departments.

Many companies also have gangs (another kind of department, more on that later) who constantly roam the halls of office buildings foraging, pillaging, and generally wreaking havoc wherever they go. (Maybe not everywhere.) You do not want to meet one of these gangs in a dark hallway.

Your clique or department will become the focus of your life, by choice or by force. Most of your working activity takes place in your department. You will experience the fun of taking part in departmental meetings, summer camp, doing time, and working late into the night.

Your department will become your home away from home. With what they pay you it may end up being your only home. You will meet many kinds of new and fascinating people at work. Some of these will become your lifelong friends, or implacable enemies.

Certainly no clique of employees can be a good department without having a good boss. Unfortunately, in most departments the choice of your boss is out of your control and thus you have to learn to deal with what you are given. Your boss will say, "I want you to do this!" then return to his office to take a nap and expect you to have it done by the time he wakes up.

Your boss leads your department at all department meetings as well as on picnics, open houses, sing-alongs, and field trips. He spends most of his time not doing any real work, but rather coming up with ways for his employees to get him a bigger salary or promoted higher up in management.

Your Departmental Name and Call

Every department has a name. Some names can be spoken freely, some are only whispered in hushed tones, and others can't be uttered in mixed company. The general rule is for a department to choose a name that encapsulates the activities of the department, such as accounting or personnel. There is also a tradition of irony by naming a department the exact opposite of its actual function, like Security or Customer Service.

More descriptive names can reveal the flavor of the work done by a department, so Accounting would become Number Crunchers, Fiddlers, Jugglers, or the Double Entry Team. These names are generally frowned upon since they don't look very good as budget headings or in annual reports to stockholders and result in more frequent audits and investigations. Similarly, they often carry negative connotations, which if spread around the company, can work in your department's favor.

You may be surprised to learn that your department will generally have a call that is descriptive of the services it provides. For instance, the whooshing sound of a mimeograph machine and the click, click, ding of a typewriter are two traditional calls for the duplicating department and typing pool.

These are a few of the most popular departmental calls.
Typing Pool or word processing.   Click, Click, vvvvvp, ding
(Originates from the days of manual typewriters, before words were processed.)

Duplicating or photocopying.   Woosh, Kechunk, Woosh, Kechunk
(Originates from the use of mimeograph machines.)

Tele-Marketing   Bbringgg, Bbringgg, Bbringg
(Repeat continually)
(Originates from the use of telephones, predating cell phones and email.)

Filing Staff   Shhh Kechunk.
(Originates from the use of filing cabinets, before hard drives.)
(Actually some hard drives do make this sound.)

Sales & Marketing (Cashier)   Piching! Phhhwhup pssh.
(Reminiscent of the days of cash registers, and when people used cash.)

Research & Development   Ka Boom!! (Self explanatory.)

Your department call is there for you to use in many official capacities. Those of you in your department will hear the call and recognize its meaning, but to others in your company, as well as to outsiders, it will sound like one of the natural background noises in an office.

Your department call can be a friendly greeting to your colleagues as you pass them in the hall. It can be used by your fellow coworkers as a warning telling everyone to stop unauthorized activity or to get back to work if your boss is coming.

It can be a signal that law enforcement officials are on their way. In times of crisis, your boss will give the call to summon everyone to an emergency departmental meeting. After work you can give the department call at a bar or outside a fellow coworker's home so they will come to meet you.

Departmental Activities

A real, functioning department will find plenty of activities to make everyone appear as if they are very busy. The main activity of your department is meetings, meetings, and more meetings. While departmental meetings are commonly held at the department's office, they can be held at departmental employees' homes, in local bars, or motel rooms.

Departmental meetings are a place where you can help your fellow employees advance in the corporate world, or where you can try to advance yourself. It is where both friendships and rivalries abound.

Departmental activities are usually planned in advance by the department head, and there is always something for every employee to do. Under a good department head, a well functioning department spends most of its time on activities that have nothing to do with daily business.

There is redecorating the office, betting pools, playing games on the office computer network, elevator racing, and other activities that are important to a well functioning department. It is at these moments, when the department is not doing any real work that departmental spirit reaches its peak.

Departmental Rules

Every department has rules that tell its employees what to do. You will find that some rules are written down such as job descriptions, regulations, and numerous useless policies. These written rules really do not govern how people actually behave in your department because, in reality, people not only ignore the rules, they often see it as a challenge to try to get around them.

The real purpose of written rules is to make your department look good to outsiders by giving them the impression that everything is going well and your department is doing what it's supposed to be doing. These rules were created by executives to avoid messy lawsuits, criminal investigations, and pesky investigative reporters.

These written rules have very little to do with what actually goes on inside your department. Rather, your coworkers are more likely to be controlled by a murky and closely held set of rites and rituals that are never written down and rarely spoken out loud.

You only find out they exist when you break them. This is why all companies (maybe not all) have so many confusing and conflicting rules. You can't help breaking a few of them, then your boss will have something he can hold over you for the rest of your life, or until you are fired.

Departmental Health

While it might seem that company healthcare plans are something relativity new, they actually predate your company going all the way back to the precursor of the corporation, the limited partnership.

Viking corporations had an employee health plan that involved outdoor sports. They played many 'away' games that sometimes got out of hand and were mistaken for invasions. The Romans had a corporate fitness program which emphasized rowing as a cardiovascular exercise. It was so effective they used it to sail around, and subsequently conquer, most of the known world.

The Greeks emphasized running as an aerobic exercise and are best known for inventing the marathon. The first marathon runner ran from Marathon to Athens and when he arrived, promptly died, making it widely popular to this day.

Some companies have employee workout facilities. This may be an actual facility like a gym with equipment and locker rooms. Or it might be the employee parking lot. Companies do this not so much for their employees well being, but because, like college sports programs, it looks good in recruiting a better class of employees. And whatever an executive might say, there is no such thing as a 'co-ed' or 'unisex' locker room.

Any good corporate fitness program is really just a devious plot to keep you feeling insecure and inadequate. Not since high school will you feel so embarrassed and humiliated in front of your peers. This is a way for the executive jocks to make their misfit underlings look foolish. It makes employees an easy target, literally. It provides the executives a means to pummel employees they don't like without the fear of assault charges because hitting them was just a sports 'mishap.'

Drawbacks of an employee fitness program.
1. Feeling even more tired in the afternoon,
2. Spending the day sitting next to sweaty coworkers,
3. Having your colleagues see just how out of shape you really are, and
4. Embarrassing 'encounters' in the locker room.

Benefits of an employee fitness program.
1. Feeling better,
2. Having more energy,
3. Losing weight, and
4. Better health. (These are what the company will say. In reality, the benefits are about the same as the drawbacks.)

Another way companies make life more complicated for their employees is through the myriad of incomprehensible forms and regulations regarding health care and health insurance. Many times the only way you will find out what's in your company's health plan is when you need some medical treatment and it doesn't cover it.

Signs your company healthcare insurance is lacking.
1. Your choices of health care plans are called rock, paper, scissors,
2. Your company medical plan refers to owees and boo-boos,
3. Your company doctor is really a Ph. D. (not an M.D.), or
4. Your 'doctor' referrers to your treatment options as eennie, meenie, miney, moe.

Things your health plan is unlikely to cover, but should.
1. In office 'massages',
2. Spa packages,
3. 'Sexual Healing', or
4. Medicinal alcohol (drinking not rubbing).

CHAPTER 4
WORK AND PLAY WELL WITH OTHERS,
OR NOT

Now that you've become part of a company, you will soon realize it has its own culture that includes corporate rites and rituals, as well as expectations and standards of conduct that will henceforth run your life. If this were not confusing enough, you will find that within your company different departments and even different individuals have their own particular culture.

You have to keep in mind that your company as a whole may have one kind of culture and your department another. Similarly, within any department certain employees are likely to typify different types of corporate cultures. This chapter is intended to help you identify the different types of corporate cultures you may encounter in your career to help you to fit in.

Types of Corporate Culture

Bunker. This culture can be the most exciting and interesting of all cultures. The Bunker culture is created by a combination of fear and panic, with an overriding air of inevitability and desperation.

Desperation drives people to strange and unusual behavior. Faced with a dilemma they cannot solve, people turn to other activities for solace. In fact, some of the best corporate parties in history were said to be held during the Soviet siege of Berlin in 1945.

Signs that the Bunker mentality exists in your department.
1. The doors and windows are barricaded,
2. The phone lines have been cut and the newspaper cancelled,
3. Department executives are often found under their desks (alone),
4. Employees are stockpiling supplies of food and water, and
5. The supply cabinet contains not only office supplies, but also mace, nightsticks, and stun guns.

This mind set is created by the constant fear of external and internal attacks. If your department is under attack from outsiders, you will feel the solidarity of fighting against the aggressors. These aggressors will serve as a rallying point for you and your fellow workers. Zealot consumer advocates, for example, can be used as a symbol upon which corporate aggression is focused.

Publicity campaigns, boycotts, picketing, low profits, or repainting the lines in the company parking lot all can create a crisis. Confronted with hellish foes that are the embodiment of darkness, you can feel a deeper unity and identification with your fellow compatriots than ever before.

If your offices are picketed, you can feel the fun and excitement of crossing through lines of hostile and rude people who would just as soon hit you as look at you. If angry mobs are regularly showing up outside your company offices, do not stand in front of any doors or windows, immerse all parcels in water, and do not answer your email in person.

If the threat is internal this changes everything. An internal attack is likely due to budget cuts based on recent analysis of your department's productivity. Like fertility rituals of early Aztec corporations, chances are your company has probably decided to sacrifice your department in order to increase productivity. As a department, you and your fellow comrades are forced to fight against the actions of the corporate turncoats who want to sell you out. While this makes life more difficult, the situation is far from hopeless.

To fight back, your department can publicize worse screw-ups by other departments, cut other department's budgets, and flood the corporate offices with customer feedback cards saying how wonderful your department is. By pooling your resources, your department is bound to be able to come up with some sort of damaging information on key corporate executives who can use their influence to protect your department from any cuts. Meanwhile, think about finding a new job. Then, stop thinking and just get a new job.

Cutthroat. This is the sort of department that gives most other departments a good name. This department has a dog eat dog environment where the sole purpose is not so much to get ahead, but to step on as many people as you can on the way. Thus, it is reminiscent of the Spanish Inquisition and many stock brokerages.

Departmental seminars are held regularly with titles such as, "How to Avoid Prosecution," "Law in Society, Ways to Get Around It," and "Corporate Immunity, A Dream Come True." They can be a boon to you if they agree with you and your policy. However, they cease to be a boon if they disagree with you, then these energetic little bastards can cause untold trouble and generally wreak interdepartmental havoc.

Keys to identifying a Cutthroat culture.
1. You hear clicking noises when you pick up your telephone,
2. When you enter the office you feel sharp stabbing pains in your back,
3. Memos calling your CEO a spineless weasel have your name on them,
4. There are hypodermic needle marks on your coffee cup, or
5. You get ticking parcels.

Intrigue and sabotage are par for the course in a Cutthroat culture. People here often compete to put in extra hours of activity (not necessarily work). It is not uncommon for your coworkers to endeavor to steal every possible idea and advantage from you. Beware of inquiries such as, "What 'cha working on" or "Maybe you could give me some advice on this project," and "Do you want me to empty your waste paper basket?"

If you fail to be of any use to your coworkers as someone to 'borrow' ideas from, or worse yet, you become a threat to their chances of success, be prepared for a bumpy ride. So always have any electrical office equipment checked before you use it. Make sure you read what you are signing or you may be signing your own death warrant, or worse, a letter of complaint about your boss.

Dedicated. In an ideal world all departments would be Dedicated. A Dedicated department is one where the employees are genuinely concerned about their jobs and doing them well. They seem to have a genuine liking for their calling.

These departments always have the interest of the corporation foremost in their mind. Or at least that's what they say at corporate meetings and inquests. Strangely enough, they usually claim that they are the only department that can save the larger organization from whatever particular threat it faces.

These are some warning signs of a Dedicated culture.
1. Employees actually come to work on time,
2. Employees only leave early on Fridays,
3. Everyone seems to enjoy their work,
4. Corporate executives actually come back from lunch, and
5. Supervisors tend to be committed.

To other departments they might seem dull, boring, or smug. As a result a Dedicated department has higher instances of getting beat up in the parking lot and having their lunch budgets taken by bigger departments.

Easygoing. This culture is the simplest and most easily identifiable workplace culture. Here standards are low and expectations are even lower. Most of the time these people are happy if anyone even shows up for work and good attendance becomes sufficient grounds for early promotion. This department has to keep up with their stationary and office supply requisitions by insisting employees take the backlog of unused supplies home for personal use.

There are several types of individuals that you will find in this type of department. Some of them will be burnouts that have dropped out of the Cutthroat, Gung Ho world for the quieter confines of the Easygoing office. Others skipped the Cutthroat and Gung Ho phase totally and would be classified as natural born louts. Unfortunately, many of these individuals, especially burnt out Cutthroats, are still self-centered, but they don't want to bother to do any work to get ahead.

This workplace atmosphere is relatively easy for most people to blend into. However, it is not recommended for those with a type A personality or for people who want to get much of anything done. This culture, as far as we have been able to ascertain, comes the closest to mirroring the culture of governmental agencies.

Signs of an Easygoing culture.
1. Executives taking naps during working hours (not a foolproof method).
2. People not coming back from lunch on Friday.
3. People leaving work early on days other than Friday.
4. When you talk to other people outside your department they say that they have never heard of your department. (Be very careful, the executives in charge of your department may have spent a long time cultivating this low profile.)
5. No one has actually told you what you are supposed to do. (When you ask, your boss gets defensive and asks you why you want to know.)

Status quo is the guiding principle of Easygoing departments and they don't want it upset. You must not alienate your coworkers or your boss by being concerned with getting anything accomplished. No department starts out in the Easygoing mode, so they will be quite protective of this Easygoing status. Remember, it takes a lot of hard work to get to the point where nothing much gets done. People will be upset if you try to undue years of work by actually achieving something.

Gung Ho. These people are committed (and they should be) to what they are doing down to the last man. They believe that what they do is essential to the company's survival and they will pursue to the bitter end the goals that they have set for themselves. If you join a Gung Ho department, you had better support the same cause. They demand loyalty to their goals and policies above everything else. Be prepared to go through long indoctrination ceremonies upon being employed here.

Departments that are Gung Ho are generally new and rapidly growing. While they have a great deal of enthusiasm going for them, they often have the organizational capabilities of a government committee. Primarily these people suffer from a narrowed scope of view accompanying their single-mindedness and tend to neglect little things in pursuit of their goals, like laws.

New corporations and departments are often found to be of this variety since most employees here are trying to prove that their existence is essential to the fate of the free world. As a result, the main purpose of this type of culture is to create as much activity as possible. If this achieves some results so much the better, but lots of activity is the main measure of success.

These are some of the warning signs of a Gung Ho department.
1. New employees have to go to boot camp,
2. You are asked to prove your loyalty by walking through burning coals,
3. Promotions are given based on surviving a trial by ordeal,
4. Executives wear camouflage, and
5. People fired from the department are literally 'fired' from the department.

The main activity of this department is to look busy and overworked to show the higher ups that it needs bigger budgets, i.e. more money. More money raises the status and importance of the department which in turn gives it more power so it can hire even more people and subsequently ask for bigger budgets and get even more money. It doesn't matter if anything is actually getting done, only that it appears so on paper. This is the only corporate principle universally adopted by government.

Narcissistic. This department considers itself essential to the smooth running of the company and everything they do as having the utmost importance no matter what others in the company really think about them. Departments of this nature take great pains in insuring that other people in the company know just how valuable it is. You often overhear departmental executives asking other executives, "Boy, how did you ever get along without us?"

Departmental executives are constantly asking everyone in their department to write letters to the CEO telling him how wonderful the departmental executives are and that they should be promoted. This is often followed by memos saying that the department needs people sending more memos about how wonderful the department is, followed by requests that everyone follow the request of previous requests.

You can easily tell a Narcissistic department's offices as the walls are often covered with mirrors so they can see themselves from multiple angles. They will display every award and trophy they have gotten since kindergarten so visitors know just how important they really are. Instead of photos of their 'loved ones,' like family members in their offices, they have photos of their 'loved one,' themselves.

Department members often have not just one, but several websites devoted to them, posted by them. They are often heard laughing, by themselves, because they thought of something clever to post on their website. They often stop in the middle of whatever they are doing to take photos of themselves to post on their website so everyone knows what they are doing, and how important it is.

Signs of a Narcissistic department culture.
1. Instead of going from 1 to 10, departmental evaluation forms go from 10 for awesome to 20 for twice as awesome,
2. Departmental higher ups insist underlings from other departments address them as sir or your eminence,
3. They are constantly stopping to take photos of themselves to post on their 'fan' websites,
4. They frequently have contests to see who has the most social media friends, and
5. During sex they call out their own name.

More often than not, this department has the effect of attracting narcissists from other departments who wouldn't have a snowballs chance in hell of getting promoted in their own departments. Since they have already been labeled as self-absorbed in other departments, a transfer to a new department will give them a pretty good chance of getting promoted before their new boss figures out what kind of employees they are. It is the abnormally high number of self-aggrandizing self-centered narcissists that makes this department culture what it is.

The Team. This culture is one in which a sense of comradeship and unity exists. It has an us versus them attitude. The Team works together against the outside world rather than backstabbing its own members. Your coworkers often say things like, winning isn't everything, it's the only thing.

A team style boss often wears a referee's whistle, chews tobacco, spits, and scratches their pants (or skirt). Corporate terms are often replaced by sports metaphors. The favorite motivational expression of your boss is "when the going gets tough, the tough get rough," Departmental offices are likely to be strewn with trophies and sports memorabilia.

Warning signs of a Team culture.
1. Before big presentations, your office holds a pep rally,
2. Departmental meetings are called huddles,
3. Employees are often penalized '10 yards' for showing up late for the huddle,
4. Employees who misbehave have to take a time out in the penalty box, and
5. The words think fast are usually followed by flying office equipment.

Always wear protection like a football helmet (or cup), with the company logo (even for women). Have lots of sports trophies prominently displayed on your desk. If you don't have a trophy you can just buy one and have it engraved to say whatever you want. People say that it's not the size of the trophy that counts, but rather how well it's engraved. Actually, in this department it really is the size of the trophy that counts.

In this system, the individualistic minded employee may find themselves put out and being accused of not playing well with others. The Team metaphor is a seductive one because it suggests an egalitarian outlook. However, while team members ideally work and play together the reality is that teams have star players, second stringers, and benchwarmers. So, which one are you?

Warm and Fuzzy. This culture is the result of a thousand years of a congenial atmosphere. Here, you will find everybody is concerned with your wellbeing and wants to make sure your life with the department is as enjoyable as possible. Executives often say things like, "we want you to be happy." Meetings often end with a hug circle.

You will know a Warm and Fuzzy culture when.
1. Executives bring freshly baked cookies from home,
2. The office has bake sales as a means of revenue enhancement,
3. Every time you come into the office an executive hugs you,
4. People are always asking, "is there anything I can do to help you?" and
5. Reports your boss likes come back with 'smiley faces' on them.

A Warm and Fuzzy culture takes a certain kind of individual to fit in. For those of you who appreciate the homey touch you will find this a rewarding and enriching atmosphere. You will notice the lovely embroidery work the corporate executives have done on the throw pillows that say things like "Office, Sweet Office." Those who do not fit in are likely to be driven insane and should seek employment in a different culture altogether.

Whirlwind. A department that is of the Whirlwind variety looks like it has just been struck by a tornado. You will find papers littering desktops and floor space alike. You will find office equipment and departmental executives scattered about the office as if some great tumult had just taken place. In fact, these departments operate on emergency status all the time. Work is pushed through just seconds ahead of deadlines and parcels are dispatched to the post office minutes before they close. These are people living life on the edge.

Ways to recognize a Whirlwind culture.
1. People run around the office rummaging through stacks of papers mumbling, "I just had it, I'm sure it's here somewhere,"
2. T-Minus countdowns for rapidly approaching deadlines are regularly given over the P A system,
3. Executives are constantly going in circles,
4. Employees regularly get blown away, and
5. This department is often featured on local weather reports.

An employee who is attracted to a Whirlwind culture loves danger and excitement. They love the feeling of not knowing whether or not the computer system will be up or if they will be able to find the financial projections. These offices are a source of constant surprise and excitement. If you are an employee here you had better to go with the flow or get blown away.

CHAPTER 5
YOUR OFFICE, YOUR NEW HOME

Your office will soon become the center of your corporate life. You are bound to have fun with other coworkers in your department's offices. You will be instructed in the rituals, traditions, and mythology of your department.

Your office is your citadel, the Bastille of your department, the heart of your company. Even though the Bastille no longer exists, your office will last forever, at least it will seem like it. As an employee your offices are a legacy to be passed on to future generations of employees. It keeps you sheltered from the elements of nature. It provides you with heat and warmth, and light even in the depths of night.

The History of The Office

The origins of the office are humble. From the time primitive man first painted corporate logos on the walls of caves the office has been the center of corporate life. The first corporations and their predecessor, the limited partnership, did not so much build their offices, as find them. A convenient cave or a sheltered grove made an ideal place to set up shop. As building techniques progressed corporate offices began to be built.

The first offices built just for corporations were more advanced structures made out of wood with thatched roofs of hay, but they lacked most of the advanced electronic office equipment we take for granted today. Over time, corporate offices came to be built in the myriad of architectural styles that characterize the great civilizations of mankind.

As time passed, offices evolved to meet the needs of their age. In ancient Egypt, corporations vied for building bigger and more impressive headquarters to show their strength and power. Sometimes referred to as 'pyramids,' these proud structures, once the hub of corporate activity, now stand empty having fallen into disrepair and decay being unable to attract new tenants. This is similar to what goes on in many major cities today.

The location and style of a company's corporate offices was often the most important decision they had to make. Locations were selected for maximum defensibility in case of a hostile takeover attempt. While corporate offices used to be built high atop inaccessible mountains for greater defensibility, today this serves only to cut down on the number of customers who stop by. Thus, a balance must be struck between defensibility and convenience.

During the relative safety and stable business environment of the Roman Empire, offices became more decorative and less practical. The Romans constructed large columned corporate plazas that included the first public restrooms called baths. Corporate employees would spend hours together in the Roman baths. This is why women today go to the bathroom in groups, they are carrying on a proud corporate tradition.

The collapse of the Roman Empire, along with many of their corporate buildings, provided a very unstable and dangerous corporate climate. Large scale office complexes disappeared in Europe as most corporations were now operating on a local basis.

In time, the economy began to grow again and corporate raiders terrorized the countryside. No one, not even limited partnerships were safe from their brutal onslaught. So, offices began to be fortified on a large scale.

This trend reached its peak in the middle ages when huge office buildings, sometimes called castles, were built with massive defenses to protect themselves from corporate raiders and door-to-door salesmen. These defenses often included tall walls, watchtowers, moats, and drawbridges designed to protect the corporate assets inside. However, over time corporate raiders developed new ways to gain control of corporate offices.

Corporate raiders used many different methods to gain access to these fortifications. Often, a gatekeeper, the forerunner of the security guard, would be paid off to open the gate to the raiders. Once past the outside defenses, a brief pitched battle usually ensued resulting in the subduing of the new acquisition. When bribery or stock offers did not work, other more cunning methods were tried.

The use of subterfuge was employed by Greek corporate raiders in raiding the corporations of Asia Minor. The most famous of these tales is the ten year attempted hostile takeover of Troy, ending in the use of the Trojan horse to gain access to Priam's corporate offices. Since then, corporations have been using similar tactics to gain access to competitors' offices using everything from industrial spies to muffin baskets.

As corporate castles were being built for the protection of corporate assets during the middle ages, undermining was developed to steal them. In its original form, undermining consisted of the corporate raiders tunneling under the walls of a corporation's offices trying to make them collapse.

Undermining is still very much in use today, but in a psychological manner rather than physically. In today's much more hostile business environment, vicious media and public relations wars are waged trying to sap the self-esteem and the will to fight from the takeover target in much more insidious ways than early raiders ever imagined was possible.

Early corporate offices were often built at strategic locations along rivers or major trade routes because they had easy access to transportation and natural resources. As these early corporations grew, they required more employees to run them who in turn built housing near their offices.

Over time, this resulted in the creation of small towns, and eventually major cities as several competing corporations, as well as supporting activities and ancillary offices, would be opened nearby. Many of the major cities we have today got their start thanks to these early corporate offices.

Your Office

Having your own workspace is very important to your overall wellbeing, as it is where you will spend most of your life. If you have a choice where to work it will be one of the most important decisions you will make. Your workspace can take many forms like an office or it could be a cubicle, a desk, a cell, or just a place to stand. You are likely to spend your time eating and sleeping there as well, so it should be comfortable so you can get a good night's sleep.

You will spend lots of time at your workspace with your coworkers and occasionally with your boss. You will spend lots of time gossiping with your coworkers about your boss and some time gossiping with your boss about your coworkers. You will while away the hours with betting pools, elevator races, field trips, and parent's nights. You will celebrate birthdays and holidays there. And if you have any free time left you might get some work done.

To find the best location for your workspace look for a clearing that is generally free of debris that could start a wildfire. It should be clear of any obstacles that could impede your career. Avoid any dead trees or over-the-hill executives, which could fall over on top of your desk. Your space should also be reasonably level so objects do not roll off your desk, but it should also let rainwater run off.

Avoid low spots where water could collect attracting mosquitoes or other office 'pests.' It should be elevated so it doesn't fill with fog that could lead to excessive condensation, or be obscured by foggy notions that could lead to excessive condescension.

Your desk should not be located where any executives could lean on you. Similarly, you should avoid leaning filing cabinets that could topple over in a windstorm (or at the next office party) and land on your desk. Your desk should be far away from your boss's office (and out of his line of sight or fire).

Your desk should be located far enough away from any sinks so that it will not be washed away in case of flash floods or situated next to large objects where lightning might strike. (Like near the legal department.)

Place your desk so your back is to the wind and the central heating system. It should also be upwind of the employee rest rooms or cafeteria. Look for a clearing where there is shelter from the elements, but which provides a gentle breeze and the midday sun so you can dry out when necessary.

Your desk should be as close as possible to the water cooler, an executive's office, or anyplace you can overhear incriminating evidence that can get you promoted. It may be helpful to have an easily accessible source of firewood. In the same way that little touches make a house a home, bring familiar items from home to leave at the office like photos, laundry, and unwelcome visiting relatives who won't leave.

Corporate offices, theoretically, should be aesthetically pleasing. So it may become necessary, from time to time, to redecorate your corporate offices. While redecorating should be left up to the taste of your particular company, it is useful to have some handy guidelines to help you determine whether or not your offices need redecorating.

1. Does the decor of your office predate the birth of most of your coworkers?
2. Is most of the furniture in your office made of primitive substances like wood?

Corporate offices are no longer just a few simple buildings. They have expanded to office complexes and even office parks. Many are the tale of corporate employees who set out for a pack of cigarettes and were never seen or heard from again.

You may have at one time or other even passed an executive who had gotten lost trying to find his way to his home office. This would explain his blank expression and disheveled appearance.

Don't worry about any of these things because it is almost certain to happen to you. Once you have a place to work it is helpful to remember where it is located so you don't get lost, but you can't count on it. Therefore, whenever you leave your office it behooves you to take some precautions, and supplies.

A few things to take with you whenever leaving the office.
1. Map and compass,
2. A roll of string,
3. Breadcrumbs, or
4. An executive who knows the way.

Each of these approaches has their drawbacks. A map and compass can help, but since the discovery of GPS no one knows how to use them. Besides, executives who think they have a magnetic personality may give false compass readings.

A roll of string is a tried and true method of finding your way back to your office, but the distance you can travel is limited by the length of your string. And you may get tangled up with other employees trying to find their way too.

Leaving a trail of breadcrumbs permits you to travel almost unlimited distances provided you have enough crumbs, but they may be eaten by executives who may also be lost looking for lunch. Taking an executive with you, while probably the most reliable option, can make you look pretty foolish, especially if he gets lost too.

Your best bet is to go it alone and if you get lost, don't panic. Climb a nearby tree or cubical and look for familiar landmarks. If nightfall is drawing near, you should probably make camp for the night. Build yourself a lean-to for shelter out of desks or cubicles to keep out of the rain or fire sprinklers.

You should make a campfire to keep yourself warm. Gather kindling for a fire using tree branches or wood office furniture (kindling may be difficult to locate as everything is made out of plastic nowadays). Look for important paper documents to shove inside your clothing to keep warm.

Things will always look better in the morning after a good night's sleep. You are more likely to recognize familiar landmarks in the daylight. Or just ask someone in the office for directions.

Chapter 6
Your Gear
and Personal Equipment

Having become an employee you might wonder what you really need to help you survive in the corporate world. Don't underestimate the benefits of sleeping around the office. So, bring two or three warm blankets, a sleeping bag, and a pillow to work.

In order to do your job you will need a wide variety of personal equipment. Eventually you will need to eat so you should bring a knife, fork, spoon, plate, cup, and bowl with you. Similarly, you want to make sure you stay clean, so bring soap (in a watertight container), washcloth, toothpaste, toothbrush, comb, towels, and a washbasin. Detergent can be kept in a watertight bottle for washing clothing. In order to avoid embarrassing misunderstandings it is a good idea to keep extra clean underwear, stockings, and other spare items of apparel in your desk.

Similarly, you will want to have on hand matches (in a waterproof case), change for the phone, personal toilet paper (in a plastic bag), cloth bandages, flashlight, binoculars, and insect repellant. A can of air freshener may be necessary in some offices in order to avoid 'embarrassing' conversations. In case you get lost you might want to have on hand a map of your office and a compass, a roll of string, and plenty of bread crumbs.

Other items you might want to have on hand include a hand saw, shovel, axe, pliers, hammer, and nails. Additionally, you will want to have a stack of post cards and stamps so you can write home.

While it has been a long standing business tradition to keep a bottle of hard liquor in your desk for 'medicinal purposes,' studies have shown that a having a bottle of 'medicine' generally results in more medical incidents than they remedy.

You will most certainly want to carry with you a copy of this guidebook. Take care of your guidebook and it will take care of you. Keep your book clean by wiping it with a soft cloth. Never immerse it in water or use any abrasive cleaners on it. Do not read your guidebook while driving, piloting a plane, or operating a nuclear reactor. Do not dissemble your book, as there are no user serviceable parts inside.

To be is to be perceived is something that has its own truth. If you want to score points with your boss and coworkers, you will want to look the part. It helps, for example, to have pictures of your family on your desk. If you have no family, borrow pictures of someone else's family. Similarly, awards and trophies always look impressive behind a desk or on a wall.

The following are some of the more common ones.
1. Sporting trophies (bowling, softball, etc.),
2. Medal of Valor,
3. Congressional Medal of Honor,
4. Iron Cross, or
5. Nobel Prize. (These have recently gotten much easier to get.)

In case of pesky inquiries or other potentially indictable investigations, having backdated letters of resignation is always a good precaution. With a backdated letter of resignation hopefully you can convince law enforcement agents that you weren't a corporate employee at the time the offenses took place.

If you have any concerns about questionable activity, put them in a memo and file it for the authorities or reporters to find in case of an investigation. This will absolve you of any responsibility and put the blame on your boss. You don't need to send these memos, unless of course you want to be fired.

To protect yourself from the threats that lurk around the office environment you may want to keep the following close by at all times.
1. Pliers,
2. Rubber hoses,
3. Bullhorn, and
4. Mace (tear gas or medieval weapon, your choice).

It is useful to keep a police band radio on hand to be monitored at all times. This will give you ample warning of any impending searches and seizures. We recommend you find a nice lightweight, well fitting protective vest or suit of armor to avoid getting stabbed in the back.

It is a good idea to have a book of employment or labor laws prominently displayed on your desk. You don't need to actually read it, just have it on your desk where your boss can see it. Studies suggest a marked improvement in the behavior of any boss when they see it.

These are some items that we do not recommend, but we have seen them in some offices like a nightstick, blackjack, stun gun, and bullwhip.

Just in case. To be prepared for any emergency we suggest the following should always be at your fingertips.
1. Emergency phone numbers (police, fire, paramedics, local embassy, etc.),
2. First aid kit,
3. Passport, and
4. Airline tickets to South America.

CHAPTER 7
LOOKS DO MATTER

Not since high school will clothes mean so much in your life as they do in the corporate world. What you wear in the office represents who you are and your uniform is part of the excitement of being a corporate employee.

Every morning, Monday through Friday, when you put on your corporate uniform you will feel ready to go out and work in the corporate world. Your corporate uniform is a constant reminder that you are dedicated to those same ideals as all other members of your company. The corporate uniform you wear makes a statement of where you've been and where you're going.

Your corporate uniform helps you to be a better corporate employee. It shows that you belong to the largest movement the world has ever known. Dressed for success like a corporate employee, you will act like a corporate employee. For many people putting on their corporate uniform for the first time is, perhaps, the greatest thrill of their life.

The History of The Corporate Uniform

The corporate uniform has changed greatly over the centuries. It reflects both the style of the company and the era it was in business. The uniform was established because early corporations soon realized that unclothed employees had lower productivity, caused a great deal of customer relations problems, and had a higher frequency of 'accidents.' As a result corporations realized their employees, by necessity, had to be clothed.

Early corporate uniforms involved little more than loincloths or coverings made of animal skins. The uniform soon evolved into the togas of the Roman corporations, the bearskins and helmets of the Vikings, and finally the modern business suit. As corporations began to specialize in the making of clothes, the corporate uniform began to change evolving into a more complex expression of the corporations themselves. This made the corporate uniform a combination of necessity, mindless tradition, current technology, and fashion fads.

One only has to look at the history of the corporation to know the importance of having proper uniforms for the conditions under which a corporation is operating. Napoleon's invasion of Russia in 1812 illustrated the dangers of local corporations not having proper clothing to withstand the corporate climate of Russian winters.

Corporate uniforms have to fit the times. Imagine the problems the loose fitting togas of Roman corporations would have in today's automated work place. One shudders to think what could result from an employee wearing a toga being sucked into an office shredder. Similarly, the success of many corporations, or their failure, is directly attributable to the suitability of their corporate uniforms.

The rise of the Hittite corporations to dominance in Mesopotamia is directly attributable to the fact that they knew how to smelt iron. This enabled them to fashion iron breastplates as a part of their corporate uniforms, overwhelming the bronze using corporations of the Sumerians and Egyptians.

We can be thankful that today the modern corporate uniform is no longer made out of iron or bronze because it was difficult to press. Instead, it consists of the suit, necktie, and dress shirt. The suit is usually dark and the shirt white making the tie the only true distinguishing feature of the corporate uniform.

While this uniform is mostly for male employees, it is often emulated by female employees along with a few variations. Some common variations include a blouse and skirt worn by female employees, mostly. Many corporations have their own unique corporate neckties that are used for corporate occasions.

The origin of the necktie dates back to the Roman Empire. Originally, corporate employees in Roman corporations found themselves stationed at quite hot branch offices. In order to prevent their employees from overheating and passing out, the Romans wore scarves soaked in water around their necks.

It took quite some time, however, for this custom to become widespread. It was not until the 17th Century that Croatian 'trouble shooters,' hired by Austria came to France wearing scarves around their necks touching off a fashion craze.

Just as neckties came to symbolize military regiments and schools, they now symbolize and represent specific companies and even separate departments within large corporations.

The suit itself has a long and illustrious history. The modern business suit is really an offspring of the medieval suit of armor.

Suits of armor were worn to prevent injury to corporate executives by hostile employees or corporate raiders. It also helped to keep spineless or sleeping executives erect and sitting upright. Thus, the suit became the backbone of corporate life. The suit of armor still had several drawbacks as standard corporate attire.

Among these were,
1. The inability of executives to sit for long hours behind a desk wearing armor,
2. The inability to bend over to pick up dropped pencils,
3. The difficulty in pressing out creases (and dents), and
4. The tendency for one's clothing to rust.

With the invention of gunpowder and bullets, the suit of armor became an ineffective means of protection. However, the mystique associated with the suit of armor continued to be associated with the executive class. Over time, armor became less bulky and the executive's uniform became more suit like.

The Modern Uniform

Now, the only remnants of a suit of armor are tie clips, stickpins, cuff links, and brass buttons. While these items are unable to stop a sword thrust or well aimed lance, or even being knifed in the back, these remaining pieces of armor still distinguish the officer class of corporate executives.

You wear your corporate uniform to all departmental and corporate functions, when you appear in an interview, or when on official corporate business. You may also wear your corporate uniform any time during National Corporation Week. You should not wear your corporate uniform during any grand jury indictment proceedings or when testifying before Congress (unless of course you are acting in the capacity of a representative of your corporation).

While there are few officially mandated dress codes, it is expected that you dress accordingly. Since it is up to you to choose how you dress to express your individuality, it is even more important that you dress like everyone else to fit in.

You should treat your corporate uniform with the respect it deserves. It is your duty to keep your uniform clean and well maintained. Be sure to check it regularly to make sure it is working properly. To keep it in good working order have it serviced regularly, making any necessary repairs. A well maintained uniform should give you years of trouble free service.

The fabric of your suit should keep you warm. This is especially desirable if your company's offices are prone to cold weather or you are experiencing budget cuts.

Your uniform should be waterproof and colorfast so it can withstand tremendous amounts of moisture without malfunctioning. This should help get you through inclement weather where there is a chance of precipitation. And it should help get you through grueling meetings where there is a chance of perspiration.

It should have adequate ventilation so you can keep your cool during times of exertion (such as disciplinary hearings). However, your clothes must also be loose fitting in order to be comfortable while at rest or while sleeping.

Your shoes should be lightweight and durable, giving you that all important edge in trying to outrun the competition. Shoes with steel tips are the best for those who are around falling objects, in sales and marketing (to stick in the door), or protect yourself from executives who just enjoy 'kicking around' their subordinates.

The following is a generally accepted set of rules to guide you in your corporate attire.

1. Never wear a suit that is more expensive than your boss's suit. (This may be extremely difficult in some cases.)

2. Never wear a suit that is cheaper than your subordinates wear.

3. No t-shirts advertising heavy metal bands or brands of alcoholic beverages are to be worn around the office.

4. Clothing emblazoned with slogans relating to your job such as, "Kiss My Assets" or "I ♥ Big Business," while showing exuberance and high spirits are considered overly excessive.

5. Similarly, other slogans such as "I ♠ My Dog" or "I ♥ ♦s" or any others deemed to be in bad taste are universally banned from corporate offices.

While it has become a competition to see who can wear the most expensive wristwatch, this is a contest you are not likely to win. Besides, a true executive never needs to wear a watch or even know what time it is. Instead, an executive will hire an assistant to tell him what time it is, which is a much more extravagant accessory than any wristwatch.

Executives never worry about being late to a meeting because they are never late. This is because a meeting never begins until they arrive. Any employee pointing out that an executive is late will, of course, need to have a wristwatch so they will be on time to the interview for their next job.

Chapter 8
Who's In Charge?

You can breathe a sigh of relief that you are a corporate employee in today's modern world. In eras gone by the corporate life of an employee has been even harder and full of more pitfalls than it does today. For instance, the Egyptian practice of burying the members of a department along with the department head, or even burying the whole staff with the CEO resulted in massive employee shortages and difficulty in recruiting replacement employees.

The modern corporate world, while not denying the possible necessity of corporate employees in the next life, holds that the staffing and recruiting problems associated with the Egyptian practice presents problems which are just too difficult to deal with.

One may wonder how executives, and most importantly the CEO are chosen. There are several rival explanations. Some scholars hold that the original method of choosing the CEO was by hereditary means. CEOs would claim to be descended from the gods and ruled by divine right. This method held that the children of the current CEO would someday become the new CEO. While this method is still used to a large extent, other methods of selection have been developed.

During the middle ages, CEOs were often chosen for their ability to lead effectively on the field of battle during hostile corporate takeovers. They were chosen for their valor and ability to carry out corporate functions, like plundering and pillaging. However, as the threat to corporations lessened over the intervening centuries, actual accomplishment and merit was abandoned as the criteria for advancement by a large segment of the corporate world.

As a result, the following methods have come into use.
1. Spinning a bottle,
2. Lottery,
3. Trial by ordeal,
4. Election, and
5. Who could promise the most to the board of directors.

The modern corporate world has evolved into a labyrinthine network of interrelationships such that no one is ever really responsible for anything. When you want something done you will find it difficult, if not impossible, to find out exactly who has the authority to allow you to do it. As a result, you will need to know how to get around those who think they are in charge, but are not and avoid those who really are in charge, but may not realize it.

Chief Executive Officer. Your CEO oversees everything that happens in your corporation. He tells your boss and all the other executives what to do. He is someone you can turn to when you need a friend. He is a source of encouragement when you need support. He is a source of cheer when you feel down. He is willing to do all of this just for you, provided you can get an appointment, get past his secretary, get past security, or even find his office, if he is even there.

He is always there just for you (and all the other employees he oversees) because,
1. He believes in the corporate way of life and everything it stands for,
2. He wants his employees to believe in the corporate way of life and everything it stands for, and
3. He gets paid more than the gross national product of many countries to do this.

The Chief Executive Officer will have many assistants with a wide variety of titles. These people dedicate their lives to the corporation and as a result they are going to make damn sure you don't screw it up. These people work very hard, taking a great burden off the shoulders of the CEO. This frees the CEO's time for more important activities such as golfing, attending political fundraisers, and testifying.

Board of Directors. The real strength of the corporation is this intrepid group of people who are behind it. They represent the stockholders who have invested their life's savings in the ultimate expression of faith in the corporate way of life. Every board member is responsible, ultimately, for the corporation's wellbeing and so they are ready to help it, or sell out to the highest foreign corporate bidder.

A board of directors often consists of descendants of the company's founders and have no real talent so they can't get a real job. A board meets for two reasons. First, it creates confidence in the shareholders that the company is well looked after. The second, and real reason is that these meetings are designed more as a ritualistic formality to keep the board of directors from bothering the executives. This keeps these nosy, meddling, busybodies out of the way of the professional management who knows how the company is supposed to be run.

Vice President In Charge of Just About Anything. These people actually do have a job, of some sort. Their real purpose is to show the stockholders that highly paid people are in charge of important aspects of the corporation. They are thus a sort of security blanket, creating the feeling that all is well within the company. After all, if a company has so many vice-presidents, it must be in good financial shape.

CHAPTER 9
GETTING YOUR BOSS TO LIKE YOU

Certainly no clique (of employees) can be complete without a leader to guide them. If you are employed in a corporation, chances are you will have to deal with a leader. Your leader, lovingly referred to as 'the boss,' will have a great deal of power over you and your advancement. Dealing with your boss is one of the single most important things you will have to do in your corporate life.

Unfortunately, the choice of who runs your life or department is out of your control so you will have to deal with whatever you are given or find a way to overthrow him and get one of your friends to be the boss. Or better yet, get the job for yourself.

Your Boss

In all corporations (probability not all) there are basically five levels in the pecking order. From the highest and most important to the lowest they are the CEO, executives, supervisors, your boss, and at the bottom are you and your fellow employees. If you are wondering why the board of directors is not here, well, just take a look at one.

Your boss is the lowest level of the managerial chain of command, just a step above the rank and file employee. As a result, he is an executive in embryo. Just separated from his beginnings as a regular employee, he is quite impressionable and still uncomfortable in his role as management. Some bosses, however, once having tasted the power of management rapidly turn into something unrecognizable.

Your boss will have his own boss or supervisor, no matter what. You can call on this person when you want to go over your bosses head, but a word of caution, your boss won't like it and you might fall (how far you fall depends how high over his head you go). Or, you might be fired.

Above your boss's supervisor are the company executives. Becoming one of these executives is your goal, your raison d'être, your destiny, and what this guidebook is all about. Executives are the folks who actually run the company (actually it is really their secretaries who do, but more on that later). Remember, whoever said it's the journey not the destination had a lousy travel agent.

Having a good boss can make your department a good place to work, or a place to hardly ever work. Your boss leads the department in all departmental meetings as well as on picnics, open houses, and field trips. You are obliged to follow your boss through the rough and the smooth, through budget cutbacks and investigations.

You must stand together for the good of your department, unless of course you can score points by going over your boss's head. At times you will be told to happily give up some of your own comfort in order to benefit your boss or department such as working late, being the fall guy, or doing time.

Your boss sometimes will have an assistant. While the basis of this selection should be with who is best suited for the job; nepotism, graft, and sexual desires often enter into the equation. An assistant will take over departmental leadership when your boss cannot be there or when he has been fired thanks to the efforts of his assistant to get his job.

One of the (many) problems you will face as an employee is getting your boss to understand you. When you first attempt this you will soon realize that your boss probably has a relatively short attention span and may not readily grasp abstract concepts or ideas. This poses a problem when it is essential that your boss understands what you are doing.

Conversely, if you don't want your boss to know what you're up to, write a long letter explaining what you are doing in copious detail. This covers you as your boss won't take the time to read it.

Life at the top is not easy. Many things demand your boss's attention and most of them have nothing to do with work. A boss has to cope with visitors, golf, and dinner parties all the time. He is also very busy thinking up ways for you to get him promoted. This makes his attention span very limited. At best you might get a few minutes of his time.

The life of your boss is full of apprehension, fear, and worry. The easy problems are already taken care of by his underlings leaving only the most perplexing and annoying problems for him to deal with, like improving his golf score.

If you want him to do something keep in mind that he cannot base his decisions on just the evidence alone. A boss is not generally motivated by the facts. More often than not, information in the form of rumors, innuendos, and gossip is going to be what determines how he will make a decision. Knowing this is advance gives you ample opportunity to think up and spread really plausible rumors and innuendos.

Getting through to your boss can be a frustrating and time consuming endeavor. When your boss is unresponsive and doesn't seem interested in anything you say or do, you may feel that you have been a bad employee. But don't, just be patient with him.

Avoid making demands or getting angry as he may run away and hide under his desk. Never scold or chastise your boss as it will not work and will likely get you fired.

If your boss is unresponsive, don't despair, it's not your fault. You might try speaking in simple one syllable words and short phrases so your boss will understand. You might use pictures that show him what you want. If you don't seem to be getting through to him, take a time out and wait awhile before trying again.

It can help to let your boss know what's in it for him.
1. Tell him it will result in more free time,
2. Tell him it will result in less actual work, or
3. Tell him it will get his name in the paper.

Use analogies that your boss can understand like,
1. Golf,
2. Sex, or
3. Other sporting activities.

These may not work if your boss is a woman. So then try these analogies.
1. Shopping,
2. Sex, or
3. Other consuming passions.

Occasionally, perhaps frequently, even incessantly, your boss may tell you "no!" You may mistakenly think that this actually means no, but few things in corporate life are as simple as that. In fact, in the corporate world, when your boss says no it often has one of these three meanings.

Simply pick the one that suits your situation best.
1. "Ask me later after I have forgotten you already asked me,"
2. "Okay, convince me that I should say yes," or
3. "Do it, just don't tell me about it."

There will come a time when your boss will be wrong (in spite of what he tells everyone) and you will know it, but he won't. When this happens, you face a dangerous decision. If you don't tell him and he finds out, he may wonder what else you're not telling him and you may be redeployed to the Antarctica branch office.

However, telling your boss he's wrong is perhaps the most perilous thing that you as an employee will have to deal with. This is not because bosses are rarely wrong, but rather it is because it is rarely in your best interest to tell him so.

You have several choices in deciding how to tell him he is wrong.
1. Tell him face to face,
2. Whisper it under his door,
3. Get someone else to tell him, or
4. Send an anonymous letter.

While telling your boss face to face may seem like the most logical approach, this course of action must be taken with a great deal of caution and tact.

Doing this can have several drawbacks.
1. Your boss will know who is telling him he is wrong,
2. Your boss may think you are after his job (he's right),
3. Your boss may fire you, and
4. You are close enough to get hit.

Whispering it under your boss's door is not a recommended way of informing him that he is wrong. First, you have to be sure your boss is in the office at the time you whisper it under the door.

Additionally, there are several other factors, which make this process more un-attractive.
1. Your voice may be recognized,
2. If your boss opens the door, it will hit you in the head,
3. People passing by will think you are stranger than they thought, and
4. You may be asked to see the company psychologist.

Getting someone else to tell your boss that they are wrong is a good idea, but rather difficult to put into practice. You must ask yourself if you are reluctant to tell your boss that they are wrong, how likely is it for you to get someone else to do it for you?

If you insist on trying to find someone to do this task for you, you may try the following enticements.
1. Promises of fame and fortune,
2. Promises of eternal salvation,
3. Promises to visit them in intensive care,
4. Promises to help them find another job, or
5. Promises to make them Secretary of State.

Finally, we are left with sending your boss an anonymous letter. This method is of the least risk to you, however, it is actually the least effective. Chances are your boss will think the anonymous letter is from one of the following groups of trouble-makers.
1. Bolsheviks,
2. Disgruntled former employees,
3. His own boss,
4. Corporate raiders, or
5. Spineless underlings. (He's actually right about this one!)

Getting Your Boss To Like You

Too many times employees think that doing 'favors' for their boss will get him to like and appreciate them. Unfortunately, the reverse seems to be true. The more subservient an employee is, the less they seem to be made of 'executive material.'

This should not be misconstrued to assume that the reverse is true. While mindlessly following your boss will not necessarily get you ahead, neither will refusing to do what he tells you to do. There are much better ways to ingratiate yourself with your boss.

If your boss is like most bosses, his behavior will eventually necessitate having an alibi be it for other executives, for members of his family, or for the authorities. Depending on the situation, you will need to think quickly on your feet to get your boss out of these sticky situations.

The following is a list of possible alibis you can employ.
1. He was with you all night. (Not recommended if you and your boss are of the opposite sex. Actually, come to think of it, not a very good idea for employees of the same sex either),
2. He was in the bathroom at the time,
3. He went home sick,
4. You were both working late at the office, or
5. You were both kidnapped by corporate raiders (e.g. Vikings).

A common misconception is that running personal errands is a good way to get your boss to like you. This is not a recommended means of ingratiating you with your boss, since it may result in you alienating yourself with your coworkers as well as with other executives. However, a busy boss often won't have time to pick up his dry cleaning, take his child to their school play, or answer depositions.

You should use this practice only sparingly, especially when it involves your boss's family. It is recommended you decline to escort your boss's spouse anywhere. Similarly, steer clear of your boss's children, especially if they are younger than ten or older than eighteen as, in either case, unhealthy and dangerous attachments can be created. Ignoring this advice could land you on a television talk show.

You may be asked to do distasteful chores for your boss. Many bosses have chores or duties that they don't particularly like to do. Some of these are obviously more distasteful than others. While you may get a certain number of points for doing them, some are simply not worth it. For example, if your boss has to fire a particularly violent coworker, who happens to know where you live, you may want to think twice about firing this employee for your boss.

Spying on your colleagues is one of the least recommended ways of ingratiating yourself with your boss. For those of you who wish to pursue it you first have to ask yourself, "do I feel like being hated and despised by my coworkers?" Now, we realize that there are those who would feel that anyone who answers "yes" to the aforementioned question is really 'executive material.'

You might try being your boss's friend. Many bosses feel that their life is a lonely and pathetic existence. (Makes you wonder why you want to be in their place doesn't it?) They are the butt of jokes and the subject of rumors that pervade the office. They are often a symbol of dislike and distrust among the employees and as a result some suffer from overly high self-esteem.

Thus, a few simple acts of kindness may transform their dull and useless existence into something with meaning. Be warned that by doing this they may develop unhealthy attachments to you. As a result, talking to or dealing with other bosses may engender feelings of mistrust or betrayal.

You may be asked to provide excuses for your boss. While this may seem closely related to providing alibis, it is an art unto itself. Secretaries are primarily employed for their skills in this area, but telephone excuses are only the tip of the iceberg in the types of excuses the average boss needs. Your help will be invaluable to your boss if you can provide good, believable excuses.

The most obvious and frequently used excuses are telephone excuses, or rather, why your boss can't come to the phone. While "he's in a meeting" is by far the most common, it is also the least believed. This is because a good executive avoids meetings and will send a lackey, like you, in his place.

The following are some other possibilities.
1. He's washing his hair,
2. He's mowing the lawn,
3. He's in the bathtub,
4. He's been kidnapped by Vikings (from a rival company), or
5. He's busy testifying.

These possibilities fulfill only a small portion of a typical boss's excuse needs. There will likely be numerous occasions where real excuses will be required by your boss. The circumstances of the problem may vary greatly as do the possible types of excuses. Have your boss select the excuse that best fits his situation, or keep trying them until one works.

The following is a list of some possible excuses for almost any occasion.
1. I thought it would work,
2. Nobody told me I couldn't do it,
3. I didn't know it was illegal,
4. I didn't know the mixture of the two was volatile,
5. I didn't know it was flammable, or
6. But the government does it.

If these excuses don't work, it's time to take it to the next level.
1. I just didn't know any better,
2. I thought it was grounded,
3. I didn't know it was loaded,
4. I didn't know he or she was loaded,
5. I didn't know he or she was under 18, or
6. I got the idea from a member of Congress.

CHAPTER 10
CREAM RISES TO THE TOP,
BUT SO DOES SCUM

There are many different types of people who rise to the top ranks of a corporation. Cream rises to the top, but so does scum. If bosses were all the same corporate life would be easy. However, not all bosses are the same because there are many different types. In fact, one might say that there are more types of bosses than actual bosses.

To help you deal with executives and bosses, listed below (in alphabetical order) are a few of the most precarious types with their distinguishing markings and recognizable habits. After all forewarned is forearmed.

Types of Bosses

The Armadillo. The boss who is of the Armadillo type is like the corporate world's little tank. While they might look armored and ready for battle, at the first sign of trouble this boss basically rolls up into a tight ball hoping to avoid getting caught up in the ensuing milieu.

This boss may look tough, but in reality is very timid. Stand up to them and they will run. If you pursue them they will bury themselves in their work or their office. These bosses are so near sighted and focused on hunting for perks that they usually won't even notice what you are up to. Be sure to check under your car before leaving work you don't accidentally run him over.

Warning signs that your boss is of the Armadillo style.
1. At the first hint of danger he locks his office door and turns off the lights,
2. He frequently goes on vacation, and
3. He has a habit of running across the road in front of cars.

The Bat. This type of boss is similar to the winged mammal they are named after. They seem to be able to see what their employees are doing even in the dark. In fact, studies have proved that you can glue their eyelids shut with almost any common office adhesive and their performance would be relatively unchanged. You have to be constantly on guard because this boss will find out what you're not supposed to be doing even while you're not supposed to be doing it.

To keep this type of boss from bothering you bring a cross and a clove of garlic to work. To get on their good side put them in charge of the chocolate covered mosquitoes. As a precaution it is always good to wear turtleneck sweaters.

Warning signs that your boss is of the Bat style.
1. He comes out at night,
2. He hangs upside down from his office ceiling, and
3. He uses echolocation to find his way around the office, (i.e. he can only find his way around the office by incessantly yelling at people).

The Chicken. The boss of the Chicken style engages in activity for the sake of activity and is constantly running around the office. When he does stop, he often perches on his desk and stares at you intently. Even with all this fluttering around, the Chicken will get very little work done, but he will make it a big deal and cackle about doing so little.

This boss always sees something to fear behind every corner and when something goes wrong he acts like the sky is falling. He easily flies off the handle, incessantly running from problems that don't exist.

Warning signs that your boss is of the Chicken style.
1. All his projects lay eggs,
2. He often pecks at things, and
3. He runs around the office like his head is cut off.

The Coach. This type of boss is most commonly found in Team departments. You will recognize that this boss thinks of everything in terms of sports metaphors. In fact, the offices of this type of boss are likely to be strewn with trophies and other sports memorabilia.

Warning signs that your boss is of the Coach style.
1. He wears a referee's whistle around his neck,
2. He shouts "think fast" followed by flying office equipment, and
3. He puts employees in the penalty box for showing up late to the huddle.

The Cowboy. This style of boss, like the western cattle driver he's named for, tends to dress like his namesake with cowboy boots, a ten gallon hat, and a big belt buckle. Whenever there is a departmental meeting he "herds" his employees to the "roundup." He likes to say things like "back at the ranch," "get on your horse," and calls his employees "lil' doggies" and tells them to "get along."

This can be a fun type of boss. You will fondly remember the evenings singing songs around the campfire. The trail rides tracking a lost department member or a rival company's employee. Meetings are often held sitting around an open fire. He likes to take his department "out on the trail." You may even be roped and tied, if you are lucky.

When this boss ropes you into something, he actually ropes you in. And when he says he wants to "show you the ropes" he actually means ropes. Since he can be a maverick in the company by making decisions his supervisors haven't approved of, look for this style of boss to be hittin' the trail sooner rather than later.

Warning signs that your boss is of the Cowboy style.
1. He likes to chew, spit, and swaggers around the office,
2. He likes to ride herd on his employees, and
3. He likes to greet others with a hardy "Yee-haw!"

The Darter. These bosses, like the fish they are named after, feel there is strength in numbers. You will notice that this type of boss will cluster with other department heads of his own type.

This process is known by many names such as schooling or herding. The instinct operating here is that in a large group, they will confuse the top executives when they are deciding whose department to cut or who to fire.

At the first hint of danger, they all take off in a dozen different directions hoping to overwhelm the sensory ability of any threatening executives. The key to dealing with this kind of boss is to isolate them from the group so they are relatively helpless and easy to get rid of.

Warning signs that your boss is of the Darter style.
1. You often find him eating or even working with his colleagues,
2. He appears nervous and fidgety, and
3. He drinks like a fish.

A variation of the Darter is the Lemming. Like the Darter, these executives operate in herds, however, they have a much different approach. While Darters try to use confusion to overwhelm the sensory ability of the corporate hierarchy, Lemmings have a rather defeatist attitude. They will all agree on one approach and simply rush headlong into oblivion. They often seem to be on the edge or can be found on the office building's ledge.

The Donkey. Some of you may be thinking that this is a polite term used to describe this type of boss. You're right. What makes this boss difficult to deal with is their stubborn insistence on you doing what they want you to do. You might as well forget trying to change their mind before you even start, or you may have to start looking for another job.

Warning signs that your boss is of the Donkey style.
1. He often brays about useless and unimportant topics,
2. He has big ears and a big mouth, and
3. His employees get a kick out of him.

The Hyena. These bosses, like their ungainly carnivorous counterpart, are not only rude, but also obnoxious. They often have an awkward, pronounced walk. While they will sometimes attack live prey, they are predominantly carrion eaters and thus attack dead or dying corporations and departments. As a result, they might prowl at night and dig up things long buried.

Warning signs that your boss is of the Hyena style.
1. He barks orders and pants,
2. He often drags dead issues around the office, and
3. You will often find him rooting around in trash bins.

The Laughing Hyena is the most obnoxious of the Hyena type of boss. He will often find serious things you say quite amusing. In order to get along with this type of boss, it is helpful to bring scraps of raw meat to the office to keep him busy.

The Laughing Hyena style boss will be amused by things you say that are quite serious like;
1. "I want a raise,"
2. "I can't do it in that amount of time,"
3. "You're a jerk!" or
4. "The building is on fire!"

The Kangaroo. The boss of the Kangaroo type is named not only for his resemblance to the Australian marsupial, but because his leadership style is reminiscent of kangaroo courts. You are often convicted before you are tried and blamed for mistakes that took place before you even joined the company.

This boss is likely to jump all over you. To keep him off your back circulate rumors that your brother-in-law is the attorney general. Also learn how to use a boomerang, just in case.

Warning signs that your boss is of the Kangaroo style.
1. He's always jumping to conclusions,
2. He gets hopping mad, and
3. He is always stuffing things down the front of his pants.
(Or she is always stuffing things down the front of her skirt.)

The Koala. This boss, like his arboreal namesake, always seems to be in rather comatose state of existence. He can sit for hours on end just staring wide-eyed at nothing in particular. Every time you talk to him, he just looks at you with a quizzical pop-eyed expression,

Beware of decorative trees in the office as this boss may drive you up a tree and out on a limb. They might hide themselves here and then drop on top of you when you least expect it. His movements and direction are so slow that they are almost undetectable. Some bosses are naturally this way, while others like the koala itself, are basically self-medicated into this comatose, bug-eyed state of virtual non-existence.

Warning signs that your boss is of the Koala style.
1. He will sit and stare into space for hours on end (not conclusive proof),
2. He smells like Eucalyptus for no apparent reason, and
3. He likes to climb out on a limb.

The Mole. A boss of this variety can be easily identified by two major characteristics, sneakiness and shortsightedness. This makes the Mole doubly difficult to deal with. They are often put into departments in order to spy on the department and report back to their superiors. This is a golden opportunity for you to share some of the 'concerns' you have about annoying coworkers you want eliminated.

Since spying is the main purpose of a mole, they are even more inept at managing a department than your average boss. As a result, they suffer from extreme near sightedness in achieving goals. Their attention span rarely exceeds where they are going to go for lunch or how long it is before quitting time. Watch your step as this boss may be digging up dirt around the office. If they get dirt on other employees, try to use it. If they get dirt on you, just brush it off.

Warning signs that your boss is of the Mole style.
1. He often bumps into walls and doors,
2. He spends most of his time underground, and
3. He likes to dig up dirt (which gets) on everyone.

A variation of the Mole type boss is the Mouse. This type of boss is more solitary and nervous. He survives by being able to adapt and blend into any surroundings. Living like a parasite off of the host company, this boss can find refuge in any nook or cranny in the office.

Since his natural defense is to remain unnoticed, bringing attention to him is the best way to deal with troublesome bosses of this variety. If you want to draw him out put a bit of cheese out, or any kind of alcohol.

The Monarch Butterfly. This boss, like the Lepidoptera he is named after, appears lovely, but is poisonous. This boss is also known as the social butterfly. They advance not so much by doing their job well, but by operating in the illustrious social circles they are trying to climb into.

They flit from department to department, all in an effort to get ahead. They will be too preoccupied with going to corporate parties and charity galas to even bother about running the department giving you a great deal of leeway to do what you like.

The best way to deal with this style of boss is to make sure their social calendar is full so they are too busy to bother with mere mortal employees. By getting them invited to all sorts of meaningless social functions, you'll have the office all to yourself. If that doesn't work get a net, a few pins, and some embalming fluid.

Warning signs that your boss is of the Monarch Butterfly style.
1. He was originally a worm,
2. Every winter he migrates to Mexico, and
3. He has the annoying habit of fluttering about the office.

The Porcupine. This type of boss is very difficult to get along with. Like the quill studded little mammal he is named after, this boss presents a great many defenses to keep employees away. Their bad habits serve to keep the employees at a safe distance from the boss and thus not posing any threat to him.

The key to dealing with this boss is to get underneath these defenses to the soft underbelly that any persistent employee should be able to rip apart.

Warning signs that your boss is a Porcupine type.
1. Bad temper,
2. Caustic sarcasm, and
3. Obnoxious personal habits. (Like smoking cigars. This is especially obnoxious with female bosses. Or perhaps erotic.)

The Puppy. This type of boss is a bundle of energy and excitement. Every day the whole world is bright and new to him. He revels in the smallest of tasks. You may notice him playfully romping around the office trying to catch a bug or intently watching one of his employees work.

This type of boss is relatively harmless, but is easily excitable and has a tendency to get under foot or scratch himself in front of company. A sharp word of admonition in a commanding tone should be used to express your displeasure with his decisions, or try using a rolled up newspaper. To get on his good side, scratch him behind the ears, or rub his tummy.

This boss is just so adorable. Yes you are, yes you are, yes you are.

Warning signs that your boss is of the Puppy style.
1. He is always excited to see you,
2. He jumps up on people visiting the office, or
3. He has a tendency to accidentally stain the rug.

The Scorpion. This type of boss has a Type A personality. Like the vicious little arachnid they are named after, they are driven to inflict pain and death wherever they go. This makes them one of the most dangerous bosses, as they will think nothing of living off the sacrifices of their employees.

These bosses should be avoided like the plague. The only benefit to this type of boss is that chances are they won't last very long. They will either advance or self-destruct.

Warning signs that your boss is of the Scorpion style.
1. He eats his young (or employees),
2. He can be a pain in the neck, and
3. When faced with an unsolvable dilemma, he will sacrifice his department.

The Sponge. This type of boss, like its namesake, is easily distinguished as an invertebrate because they have no spine. This lack of spine can lead to immediate benefits, but long-term problems.

It may seem like a dream come true when your boss agrees with all of your ideas. However, this exuberance will quickly turn to disappointment when you realize that he has also given his support to every other employee as well.

He simply can't or won't say no. Even worse, he will tell you and your fellow coworkers to work it out amongst yourselves. Other examples of Sponge like behavior include borrowing money from subordinates and absorbing any nearby liquids (such as bottles of scotch or whiskey).

Warning signs that your boss is of the Sponge style.
1. He absorbs everything around him,
2. He lets others pay for everything, and
3. He drinks practically everything in sight.

The Teddy Bear. Like the puppy, this type of boss is loveable and huggable. The Teddy Bear is easily moved to emotion. You will find their emotional attachments to their employees are a source of both inspiration and suffocation. Their slogan is, "have you hugged your employee today?"

They tend to be less active in the winter, spending it in a sleep-like dormant state of existence. This is a good time to get what you want as they are less likely to be aware of what's going on around them as they spend most of the time hibernating in their office.

Warning signs that your boss is of the Teddy Bear type.
1. They tend to be furry (i.e. lots of body hair), (even with some women bosses),
2. They tend to appear overstuffed, and
3. They tend to sit quietly in the corner and smile for no apparent reason.

The Viper. The boss who is a Viper brings new meaning to the phrase 'snake in the grass.' This boss is both venomous and scaly, but lacks the style and bright coloring characteristic of the reptiles he's named after.

Because of his venomous nature, you should exercise caution in your dealings with him. It is safest to stay as far away from these types of bosses as possible as they can be vindictive.

Warnings signs that your boss is of the Viper style.
1. He likes to sink his teeth (fangs) into things,
2. He doesn't so much walk as slither into the office, and
3. He often tries to swallow tasks bigger than his head.

The Weasel. The boss who is of the Weasel variety is one of the most savage and ruthless of all the bosses. While you may think that they get their name because of their treacherous and vile behavior, the true origin of the name comes from their cruelty and savagery. A boss of the Weasel variety will want to gut and destroy a department simply for the sake of gutting it far beyond the needs of the corporation to become more efficient.

Never show any weakness to this boss because they will attack anything they see as vulnerable. They go directly for the jugular with little provocation. In an argument with other types of bosses, the Weasel usually wins. This is important for you to know not from a business standpoint, but rather to win bets around the office.

Warning signs that your boss is of the Weasel style.
1. He often comes to the office soaked in blood or cologne,
2. He often intently eyes live chickens, and
3. He has been to law school.

Chapter 11
Getting Your Coworkers To Do
What You Want

By now you probably will have shrewdly noticed that you are not alone at work. There are a wide variety of people who share your workspace and company offices. These people are your peers, your contemporaries, your coworkers, and your enemy. Unfortunately, you will have to learn to deal with them because you will find it nearly impossible to avoid them.

At some point in your corporate life you will have to ask someone to do something. When that time comes you will want to be ready for it. This chapter is designed to familiarize you with some of the more common types of coworkers that the corporate world has created.

In the first known corporations, commonly referred to as hunting and gathering limited partnerships, there was little division of labor. Employees were either hunters or gatherers. The need to carry on corporate activity to stay alive precluded a need for executives or any finer division of labor.

However, with the Neolithic Revolution, mankind and the business world started down the path to the specialization of labor that we have today. Now, we have a vast panorama of occupations. Listed below are some of the more common corporate employees you will no doubt encounter.

Secretaries. You will soon realize it is not so much the executives who run things, but the secretaries. Secretaries control the day-to-day operations because they are responsible for implementing or disseminating orders from the top of the chain of command because executives are too busy playing golf or testifying.

Since it is secretaries who control the flow of information and determine who gets to see whom, they can help or hinder your chances of becoming an executive. They may inadvertently make clerical errors that can ruin your life. Thus, it behooves you to be as nice as possible towards these corporate guardians.

Mistreating secretaries can result in,
1. Never getting another phone message ever again,
2. Your bookies calls are accidentally forwarded to your boss,
3. Photocopies of embarrassing personal correspondence or medical files begin to appear around the office,
4. You accidentally get transferred to the Lebanon, Baghdad, or Somewhere-nobody-ever-heard-of-stan branch office, or
5. Your company personnel photo appears in post offices.

Benefits from being nice to secretaries include.
1. Calls from rival coworkers' important clients get transferred to you,
2. Your personnel file 'accidentally' gets forward for review for a promotion,
3. You 'accidentally' get transferred to the New York or Paris branch office,
4. You get advanced notice of surprise locker inspections, or
5. Rival employees company I.D. photos began appearing in local post offices.

What should you do to be nice to secretaries you ask? Bring them little gifts, run short errands for them, offer them sex, or wash their car.

Filing clerks. In many offices this function is taken over by a secretary, but in many corporations these exist as a separate job classification. They can be found in many departments like Human Resources. These backroom underlings have a great deal of power because they control information and are important to the smooth running of any company.

Filing clerks are very useful in helping you become an executive and to sabotage your enemies within the company. With any luck your rivals' proposals can accidentally be filed where no one will ever be able to find them again.

It is filing clerks who are often the last bastion of corporate defense. As investigators or revolutionaries are battering down the front door it is these stalwart clerks who are busy shredding incriminating documents, or dropping them out the window to waiting reporters.

Consequences from mistreating filing clerks.
1. Your personnel file 'accidentally' doesn't get forwarded for review for a promotion.
2. Your personnel file gets mixed up with another employee's file and your file is sent for disciplinary action,
3. Every project you have worked on for the last twelve months isn't where it's supposed to be in the files.
4. Your personal file containing embarrassing person information (fabricated, of course) 'accidentally' ends up on your boss's desk.

Benefits of befriending filing clerks.
1. Your personnel file 'accidentally' gets forwarded for review for a promotion.
2. Your personnel file gets mixed up with a rival employee's file and his is sent for disciplinary action, instead of yours,
3. Every project your rivals' have worked on for the last twelve months isn't where they're supposed to be in the files.
4. Your boss's file containing embarrassing personal information 'accidentally' ends up on your desk.

Accountants. These stoic employees are perhaps among the most important to your success, which makes them one of the most dangerous because accountants are often difficult to like.

However, they wield a great deal of fiscal and monetary power. They can be invaluable allies and implacable enemies.

Results that can accrue from mistreating accountants.
1. You were accidentally put down as having no dependents for tax purposes,
2. Your paycheck is lost somewhere in the computer system, or
3. It appears as if you've been embezzling funds you've never seen.

Benefits that can accrue from making friends with accountants.
1. You are put down as having the maximum number of dependents for tax purposes,
2. You worked more hours than you thought, or
3. An accounting error undervalued the amount of money you were supposed to have earned giving you a big bonus.

Janitorial Staff. The janitorial staff keeps your company and your workspace from being totally overrun by its own refuse. Without janitors and cleaning crews your offices would soon fill with memos, reports, red tape, and other rubbish thoroughly clogging them beyond any use. You may think their job is to simply clean up your messes. This is a common misconception that can result in you drowning in your own waste.

Consequences of mistreating janitorial staff.
1. Never having your wastebaskets emptied,
2. Your important reports 'accidentally' get tossed out in the trash, or
3. Your office has become the entire building's landfill site.

Benefits from making friends with janitorial staff.
1. Always having a clean office,
2. Having rivals important reports 'accidentally' tossed out in the trash, or
3. Having important or incriminating papers which rival employees 'threw out' end up on your desk.

Your relationship with the janitorial staff can bring back some of the most exciting moments of your childhood. Every day can be like Christmas Eve as you wait for Santa Clause to come. You will be amazed by the changes in your office and your good fortune if you leave little presents for the janitorial staff, like milk and cookies or bottles of hard liquor.

Sales and marketing. The sales and marketing personnel are among the most benign, but obnoxious coworkers you will encounter. Thankfully, they exude little control over your everyday life. Unlike other kinds of coworkers, sales and marketing personnel only have a limited number of ways they can make your life miserable. At worst, if you get them mad your personal home phone number is 'accidentally' posted on the company website as the 24 hour hotline for the complaint department.

The best you can hope for is that your boss's personal home phone number is 'accidentally' posted on the company website as a 24-hour number for the consumer complaint department, driving him insane and opening the way for your promotion, and probably his as well.

Legal department. These people can suffer from a narrow point of view. Motivated by their single-mindedness they tend to neglect the little things in pursuit of their goals, like the law. They can be a boon to you if they agree with you. However, if they disagree with you, these energetic little nitpickers can cause untold trouble and generally wreak inter-departmental havoc.

Results that can stem from mistreating legal staff.
1. Having your name found on incriminating documents,
2. Always having to testify,
3. You have become the fall guy for your boss's 'creative' accounting, or
4. Discovering your office romance is not of 'legal' age.

Benefits that can result from making friends (they don't usually have many) with legal staff.
1. Having your rival's name found on incriminating documents,
2. Never having to testify,
3. You have become the beneficiary of your boss's 'creative' accounting, or
4. Not having to worry if your office romance is of 'legal' age.

Security Guards. The title security guard is a misnomer in many companies. They don't so much secure anything as make everyone feel insecure. While to a large extent the term, 'insecurity guard' has not caught on, it may be a more appropriate title for this type of personnel. Security guards are often employed because the executives feel insecure. This may be due to internal threat, external threat, or more often than not, both.

The following are types of internal threats security guards are employed to protect against.
1. Crazed or disgruntled employees mutilating valuable corporate property,
2. Crazed or disgruntled employees mutilating valuable corporate executives,
3. Wholesale looting of office supplies (this occurs anyway), and
4. To keep the board members out of the building.

The following are types of external threats security guards are employed to protect against.
1. Corporate takeovers (they are actually of little use in this capacity),
2. Natural disasters (ditto),
3. Auditors (ditto), and
4. The 'anti-corporate rabble' out to destroy everything the corporate executives hold sacred (ditto).

All too often the people employed as security guards contribute to the acceptability of the term 'insecurity guards' as they may occasionally fit the following descriptions.
1. Crazed homicidal maniacs,
2. Former disgruntled employees,
3. People with felony records, and
4. People who like guns and uniforms, but couldn't get into the armed forces.

The reaction of other office personnel to security guards does not always engender feelings of safety, but rather of insecurity.

There are several factors that contribute to these feelings of insecurity.
1. People standing around the office.
2. People standing around the office in uniform,
3. People standing around the office watching every move you make, and
4. People standing around the office with guns.

CHAPTER 12
TEMPORARY HELP,
PERMANENT ENTERTAINMENT

Temporary employees are occasionally needed to fill vacancies in your department due to illness or accidental death. Temporary help is often looked at as the equivalent of substitute teachers in school. They are not so much hired for doing work as for providing entertainment.

The History of Temporary Help

Modern temporary help is a far cry from his early origins. Temporary employees have been known by many names throughout the ages including hirelings, free lancers, soldiers of fortune, and the all-pervasive mercenaries. Historically, hiring temporary help has been a two edged sword. While at times they have actually succeeded in helping a company run better, more often than not temporary help has worked to a company's disadvantage.

To illustrate the problems associated with hiring temporary help one need only look at the struggle of Celtic corporations to maintain their market share after the withdrawal of critical Roman investments in Britain in the 4th century after the bankruptcy, or fall of the Roman corporate headquarters. Local Celtic companies were being put out of business by competition from the Picts and Scots' limited partnerships.

In order to regain their market share, the Celtic companies in Britain turned to temporary help from several Germanic firms, like the Angles and the Saxons. However, once they were established rather than helping the Celtic companies in Britain, the temporary help got drunk and generally pillaged the countryside. They invited their colleagues over from Europe and within a matter of a few hundred years they overran Britain establishing their own business associations.

Another instance of temporary help run amuck happened during the Thirty Years War when their employment was expanded on a scale never seen before. What began as competition between Germanic Protestant upstart firms and the Roman Empire Corporation escalated into an all out price war.

With the potential of a Roman reorganization imminent, Danish CEO Ferdinand II sought to gain market share in Germany. In 1626, to establish new locations, Ferdinand hired Swedish executive recruiter Albrecht of Wallenstein to find him temporary help.

Once hired, Wallenstein added over 100,000 employees loyal to him gaining large market segments in Germany and then masterminded a hostile takeover of the Danish head offices. He evicted Ferdinand's employees from the territory that his 'temporary' employees now occupied.

Because of temporary help gone wild, in less than ten years the Danish companies were out and Swedish corporations had established an all time high in market share in Europe.

Modern Temporary Help

While temporary hiring is now done on a much smaller and therefore less dangerous scale, temporary help presents its own unique problems. The following are some guidelines in dealing with modern temporary employees, commonly called temps because they tend to run either hot or cold.

When the boss first brings a new temp to the office the older employees may react with hostility or resentment. They may think that the boss is trying to replace their old colleague with a newer, younger model. This can engender feeling of misgivings about the temp. They may refuse to work with or even talk to the new temp. They may feel that this is just another in a long line of 'temps' the boss brings to the office.

The older employees may feel that soon the boss will lose interest in his new temp and they will never see them again, so why should they get attached. This can lead to feelings of animosity where the older employees feel they need to get the temp in trouble so their boss won't like the temp anymore and get rid of them.

As a rule, you should always treat a temporary employee with the same respect you treat your coworkers. However, it is difficult to overlook the fact that you do not have to worry about long term retribution or retaliation from a temp since they are not going to be around for very long.

This can serve, for some, as an incentive to pull pranks on them because chances are they will not be able to exact revenge for harmless office high jinks. In this way temps are a bit like substitute teachers in high school. Not so much a means of getting any real work done as much as a source of entertainment.

In welcoming temporary help to the office it is customary to show humor. While destructive humor is smiled, we mean frowned, upon it is possible to make their welcome something of a highlight of an otherwise boring and tedious day.

While there are many creative ways to lighten up those first tense moments in the office, the following sorts of jokes or pranks should be avoided.
1. Anything that involves physical injury,
2. Anything that involves destruction to office property, and
3. Anything involving flammable substances.

Keeping these guidelines in mind, you should be able to avoid any lawsuits or other unfortunate results of misunderstood office pranks.

Popular office pranks fall into one of the following categories.
1. Disorientating the temporary employee,
2. Tampering with the employee's office equipment, and
3. Modifications to office furniture.

Since they don't know what they should be doing, temps learn by imitating the other employees around them. This is why they can sit for hours just watching their coworkers do their work. Disorientating a temporary employee is rather easy to accomplish since they are in a new and unfamiliar environment. On agreement of your coworkers, one or another of you can pretend to be an executive and think of unique and humorous tasks for the temporary employee to undertake.

Being unfamiliar with the office, the temporary employee will not notice things like the nameplates on the rest room doors being exchanged, or certain offices and rooms being mislabeled. How many times has the temporary employee been embarrassed by accidentally taking their lunch into their boss's office thinking it was the employee lunchroom?

You can use a temporary employee's lack of familiarity with departmental customs as a source of good humored mischievous fun. You can set the office clock back half an hour so they will show up late to a meeting with their boss. Afterward, be sure to set it ahead so when the temp tells their boss they were late because the clock was wrong, when he looks, it is set to the correct time. You can tell the temp Thursday is 'toga Thursday' and leave an official memo where they can see it. When they are the only one to show up at the meeting with the CEO wearing a bed sheet, hilarity will ensue.

Tampering with a temporary employee's office equipment can provide hours of entertainment. It can be even funnier when the tampering is tailored to their job activities. Popular pastimes have been changing computer keyboards from the popular Qwerty mode to the more interesting Dvorak mode. This results in page after page of totally incomprehensible text. With any luck, it will take several documents for the error to be realized and hilarity should ensue.

Another time honored tradition is rewiring office equipment or modifying office furniture so they do not function as a temporary employee thinks they should. However, doing this may result in the inability to ever use these items properly ever again and may result in increased liability or culpability on part of the company for any 'accidents' that might result.

A word of warning here, tampering with office property is not recommended nor should you participate in any actions that would be rude, obnoxious, or discourteous to any temporary employees, coworkers, or executives or cause damage to corporate offices or equipment, unless it's really, really funny.

THERE'S A TYPO.

CHAPTER 13
HANDLING YOUR EQUIPMENT
AROUND THE OFFICE

Once you become part of a clique of employees there will come a time when you will find yourself in the awkward spot of actually having to communicate with someone else. While face-to-face communication may seem like the most natural and logical thing to do, it can be considered a rude and offensive breech of office conduct. This is why the corporate office has so fully embraced the use of office equipment, so executives don't have to actually see their employees in person.

Your office is filled with many complex and costly pieces of office equipment. This equipment is very expensive and must be used to justify its cost. If you do not use this equipment your boss is bound to become offended and upset.

All that equipment in the office is not just for show (actually it is there for show), but also to be used. In fact, most departments feel the more you use them the better since it shows that the department is actually doing something. As a result, rather than talking with people face to face you will be forced to communicate with people not only across the continent, but just a few doors down from your office by time consuming and ineffective means.

Predecessors of modern communication devices included many unique and in-novative attempts to send messages between company offices. Early Native American companies employed the use of smoke signals for transmitting memorandum.

This method had several major drawbacks.
1. Messages had to be of short duration,
2. The branch office had to be close enough to see the signals,
3. They were open to hackers and government surveillance, and
4. They violated no smoking laws.

The Romans and Greeks used a network of runners who would pass a memo in a relay race across the countryside from one company location to another.

Like the Native American system, this system too had its drawbacks.
1. While the length of the message could be greater it required more employees, thus long distance communication was quite costly compared to local service,
2. Due to the practice of killing the messenger bearing bad news (such as fourth quarter losses), it became difficult to recruit staff.

Memos. These are the most traditional form of corporate communication. While memos predate the more technologically advanced telephone and computer systems, they are still a corporate mainstay. As the technology used in corporate communications has progressed, it has been solely for the purpose of creating more expensive and complicated ways of sending memos.

After all, messages left on answering machines and emails are just upgraded versions of the traditional memo. Actually, it was the need to send more memos to increasingly evasive employees who had learned to dodge phone calls and disable answering machines that led to the invention of email, texting, and the internet.

The origin of the memo can be traced back to primitive man's first attempt at the corporation, the limited partnership. Sending memos was a time consuming and bulky process as the first memos were chiseled in stone or written on clay tablets. These stone tablets were very durable, but were expensive to mail and didn't fit well in filing cabinets. They also offered little privacy as they keep turning up all over the countryside embarrassing corporate executives.

These Rune Stones of early Viking corporations are still being dug up in farm fields since they were almost impossible to discard as they won't burn or go through shredders. However, being quite bulky and heavy they did make excellent paper-weights, unfortunately paper had not been invented yet.

The paper memo, as we know it, has its roots in the clay tablets of Assyria, Babylon, and the ancient Greeks. However, its current form began to solidify both in ancient Egypt and China. In Egypt, the use of papyrus and in China the development of wood pulp paper made the memo an easier and lighter means of corporate communication. Given the rather cold and drafty corporate offices of this era, paper memos had one other benefit over clay and stone memos, they were burnable.

The flammability of the paper memo provided a way to avoid the embarrassment of early Viking corporations because memos could now be easily destroyed so they don't fall into the hands of corporate rivals. However, this development proved to be a two edged sword.

While it was possible to supplement office heating with memos, it also led to the rather unfortunate loss of key corporate documents. The burning down of the library at Alexandria meant the loss of untold corporate documents and is rumored to have been started by temporary employees trying to warm up their lunch.

This established a tradition that thoroughly ingrained the memo as the lifeblood of the corporation. Memos are sent about office paper requisitions, birthdays, births of kittens or puppies, the winner of the office betting pool, and other essential corporate business. While there have been attempts by corporations to curtail the use of memos, the memo has resisted both corporate opposition and the introduction of new technologies to remain the mainstay of the corporate world.

Correspondence. Correspondence is, simply, a more advanced and complicated form of the memo. A letter is nothing more than a very large memo with a heading and a signature. While memos are usually used for inter-office communication, correspondence is used to communicate with those people in the outside world or in other corporations. It was found that outsiders often could not understand the meaning of corporate memos so in order to be able to communicate with people outside of the corporation, it was necessary to explain things in greater detail.

The formality of the letter is designed for the sole purpose of impressing the recipient. It demonstrates that the sender knows how to use proper language and grammar. It shows the recipient the respect the recipient thinks they deserve. This gives the recipient the perception that the sender is competent and knows what they are doing while having everything under control. This is the exact opposite of email.

Telegrams. There was a time when these were the latest in high tech, high speed communication. Their one big contribution to society was that they spread the use of the memo from the corporate world to the rest of society. Not only did corporations send telegrams, but now people learned how to send memos announcing births, weddings, and declarations of war. Much like email works today. This had a great effect in popularizing the corporate way of life and making the corporate world a less foreign and forbidding place than it had once seemed to many average citizens.

There was a time when the telegram was cutting edge, state of the art technology, so telegram companies could charge whatever they wanted. Much like many companies do today. Their high cost encouraged brevity in sending memorandums so people tried to cram as much information into as small a message as possible. This led to some unfortunate misunderstandings.

One famous misunderstanding over a telegram led to the US declaring war, which may have been a bit of an overreaction. Much like what happens today. In 1917 the German foreign minister sent a telegram to the German representative to Mexico. Wanting to keep the US out of the war in Europe, Germany proposed a limited partnership with Mexico suggesting they declare war on the US to keep them busy and in return they would get Arizona, New Mexico and Texas back.

The British discovered this potential merger and informed the US who, after careful consideration declared war on Germany, entering World War I. In true corporate fashion, Germany contended that it was all just a "hypothetical" idea floated by a "disgruntled" employee.

Telex. Due to the high cost of telegrams, and their potential to fall into the wrong (or right) hands, the corporate world searched for a cheaper means of sending lengthy and unimportant memos. Technology would soon provide the answer with the introduction of the telex.

The telex system was designed to allow companies to send their own telegrams across country without the expense of transcribers who could be bribed by rival companies. Because it allowed a greater volume of memos to be generated in a shorter period of time, it was quickly embraced by the corporate world. Thus, the telex became a quicker way to send memos across longer distances resulting in fewer declarations of war.

Typewriters. While the need for entertainment and to waste time has led to corporate employees embracing a plethora of various technologies, none have changed the office like the typewriter. The need for corporate employees to communicate with one another without having to see each other face-to-face actually predates the corporation going all the way back to the limited partnership.

However, it took until the 18th century for employees to realize that if you could tell a coworker or executive something without being close to them you are less likely to be hit, beaten, or garroted. This realization and its ability to turn out reams of useless documents made the typewriter wildly successful in the corporate world.

Once corporate employees learned how to use the typewriter, the time saved by not having to write things out by hand could now be channeled into a tremendous increase in the time spent with parties, coffee breaks, betting pools, and other useless time filling tasks that are so commonplace in the corporate world today.

Computers. Computers are the newest and, for many, the most annoying addition to the office. They are basically just a much more expensive typewriter which takes hours to set up, instead of a only few minutes just to type a simple memo which is why they are wildly popular with business and government alike. Unlike the manual typewriter, they are often down and fail to work when the power is shut off for non-payment of utilities resulting in more frequent coffee breaks.

As such, you will eventually be forced to come face to face with one of these imposing and threatening devices. The first rule is to remain calm. Computers can sense fear. You have to show the computer who is boss. Remember, your computer is more afraid of you than you are of it.

You will soon realize that your company has hired computer specialists and may even have a computer services department. There are thousands (maybe not thousands) of computer and software manuals designed for one purpose, to make you even more confused.

After all, if regular employees easily understood and grasped the use and handling of computers, the computer specialists would all be out of a job. Thus, it behooves these departments to make the computers a mysterious and forbidding force to be reckoned with.

Early corporations had their own form of computer specialists. They were known by many names like shamans, acolytes, and oracles. Whatever they were called, they served to mystify the other members of the corporation. The druids, for example, would hold festivals to invoke the changing of seasons knowing full well that the seasons would change regardless of how many geese or small mammals (or corporate employees) they sacrificed to invoke the change of seasons.

However, they had to justify their existence since they didn't actually produce anything that could be used by the corporation. So they shrouded their jobs in ritual and pretense. In the same way, computer specialists (and legal departments) have generated a mystical aura around what they do.

Copy machines. The photocopy machine has been, perhaps, the most revolutionary device to be introduced into corporate offices. Before the copy machine, documents had to be tediously and laboriously copied by hand. From the scribes of the pharaohs to the monks of the middle ages, duplicating was the sole responsibility of a select few.

This system had its drawbacks. Confidentiality was virtually non-existent since someone had to read a document to copy it. While this augmented the revenue of copyists, (via extortion) it made life difficult for corporate executives.

The forerunner of the copy machine, the mimeograph, was not much better. It did have the advantage of using toxic chemicals, which were inadvertently inhaled by those using it. The result was slightly medicated, but generally happy employees.

The copy machine has several distinct advantages over the old system of scribes and copyists.
1. They don't have to be paid,
2. They don't complain,
3. They don't make mistakes,
4. They don't take up as much office space,
5. They don't get tired, and
6. They can't blackmail you.

Given these obvious advantages the copy machine quickly spread throughout the corporate world. The modern copy machine puts the ability to produce memos, charts, pictures, copies of various parts of anatomy, and reams of useless information into the hands of every employee relatively quickly. (Warning: It is not recommended to attempt to photocopy any part of human anatomy on any copy machine where the document moves back and forth.)

While copy machines cannot black mail you, they put into the blackmailers hands an easy and efficient way to make copies of incriminating pieces of evidence to be mailed or faxed to the blackmailee at the blackmailer's leisure while keeping the original document safely locked away.

Shredders. The development of the shredder can be seen as a direct result of the copy machine. Originally, useless corporate documents were merely discarded. These corporate records, commonly known as Rune Stones, proved bulky and did not fit very well in filing cabinets, so they ended up littering the countryside. These tediously huge documents chiseled into stone by early corporate employees are still turning up all over the world. Every so often a farmer in Scandinavia digs up some discarded corporate memo or document.

With the use of paper, fire became a method of easily disposing of corporate documents. Unfortunately, when the sheer volume of corporate documents increased, fire became an increasingly dangerous method of disposal. The burning down of the library at Alexandria is one such unfortunate incident.

The copy machine and computer printer have greatly compounded this problem. The sheer volume of paperwork produced by the modern corporation would result in devastating firestorms of epic proportions if fire was still the only way to dispose of them. Certain corporations have tried other methods such as flushing documents down toilets, but all have proved ineffective.

Simply throwing the documents away would leave them fair game for the spies and saboteurs that every really paranoid executive knows are out there lurking to find out how much coffee his department is using. This and other top secret, proprietary information is now destroyed by shredding it.

Similarly, it was often difficult to dispose of incriminating or embarrassing documents, especially on short notice. The shredder has allowed corporate executives the ability to destroy embarrassing or incriminating documents while the auditors are busy summoning the police or a locksmith to gain access to the offices.

Given enough delaying tactics and a good strong door, most documents can be destroyed on relatively short notice. Be warned, however, that this is not fool proof. When presented with political zealots or zealous prosecuting attorneys with lots of free time on their hands (or paid by the hour), some shredders do not fully obliterate the document allowing these people to 'sew' them back together.

Thus, we recommend a really high quality shredder. One that does not so much shred as pulverizes. They are really worth the investment and may mean the difference between indictment and acquittal due to lack of evidence.

While unlicensed and inappropriate use of office shredders is not recommended, it has become a popular pastime in the modern corporate office to find out what exactly can and cannot be shredded. Use caution, any articles of clothing this is attempted on should not be attached to any employees.

Security cameras. While management may tell you that security cameras are being used to protect your offices from burglary and such, they can just as easily be used to monitor your activity. The earliest form of security camera was actually another employee. Throughout history, they have been known by names such as guard, sentinel, or stool pigeon.

These guards were hired to ensure that work was actually getting done. In reality, they had several drawbacks. Despite the necessity of paying them, they were also available to other bidders, via bribes, and often proved unreliable. The security camera, on the other hand, put in the executives' hands the ability to monitor their employees without them even noticing it.

Combined with video recorders, a great deal of supervision can take place without the employee's knowledge. It also allows for a permanent record of various interoffice 'transgressions' for use at upcoming departmental meetings, disciplinary hearings, office parties, or to post on the internet.

Centrex systems. Telephone systems of various types have been incorporated into the corporate world. These phone systems conveniently put at your disposal access to any of the office telephone lines. With a little ingenuity and background in electrical engineering, you can eavesdrop on any conversations taking place from your offices. An industrious and conscientious employee can think of all sorts of interesting applications for this like settling bets, finding scandals, and blackmail.

The real purpose of a telephone system, however, is obvious to any person who has ever tried getting a hold of someone at a corporation or government agency. Before telephones, people who wanted to complain about something or who wanted to talk to an executive had to go directly to their office and speak to them face-to-face. This explains why early corporate offices were generally fortified. Castles, for example, with a series of high walls, moats, and drawbridges that made it virtually impossible for people to just 'drop in' on unwilling corporate executives.

The telephone was invented to protect executives from unwanted intrusion by ordinary folk. Now, when someone calls to complain, they can be put on hold for hours or 'accidentally disconnected.' While this does not eliminate all the troublemakers it weeds out all but the most determined.

Similarly, it is almost impossible to deny that someone is not in the office, if the person trying to get a hold of them is physically in the office as well. However, someone on the telephone can easily be told "he just stepped out for a minute," or "I'm sorry, he's busy testifying." It is far easier to avoid people via the telephone than it is in person, which is why it was invented in the first place.

Answering machines. These electronic marvels, along with answering services, were introduced into the office as a means of not so much cutting costs or ensuring effective communication, but for their ability to be annoying. It also weeds out messages from people who are alienated by trying to talk to a machine.

While it is considered rude not to leave a message when you reach an answering machine, you can express your displeasure with having to talk to a machine by randomly dropping syllables and words out of your message or by speaking very slowly or rapidly. With any luck it will be weeks before the repairman determines there is nothing wrong with the answering machine.

Answering machines are considered more dangerous than memos. While one can disavow having sent a memo, providing one did not sign it, it is almost impossible to disavow having left a message on an answering machine. Similarly, there is no anonymity with an answering machine. This is why the answering machine will never replace the memo.

While a person may anonymously send a "you suck" memo to a certain executive or a coworker that gets on their nerves, it is highly recommended that you do not leave "you suck" messages on answering machines. It is rather hard to deny you left the message when it's in your own voice. Memos offer both anonymity and deniability.

Fax machines. The fax machine is the most exciting thing to happen to memos since the invention of paper. It allows not only text to be sent as part of a memo, but exact copies of whatever documents you want sent. Single handedly, the fax machine has contributed to the renaissance of useless inter office communications. Not only can the winner of the office betting pool be announced, but their picture can be sent to corporate offices around the world.

The fax machine made it possible to send things from office to office that had previously only been dreamt of by employees. Not only could "you suck" memos be sent from fax machine to fax machine, but diagrams and illustrations explaining how proposed actions to 'remove them from the office' would be carried out could also be included.

You can impress your friends and relatives who visit you at work by telling them you're faxing something to China when, in reality, you're just faxing it to the office down the hall.

Electronic mail. With the introduction of the computer it became possible to send memos via this new electronic medium. Computers are perhaps the most impressive looking of all office equipment, which is why they are so widely used.

It actually takes longer to write and send an email than to simply pick up the telephone and call someone. However, email has the advantage of not having to actually talk to someone. Most of the time office computers are not actually used for any real office work, but rather used primarily to impress clients.

Electronic mail does one thing that neither the memo, the telex, or the telegram do, they take paper out of the loop. Due to this shortcoming electronic mail is generally frowned upon as it results in a precipitous drop in paper consumption.

To combat this problem most offices require printing out all electronic mail. This results in the consumption of just as much or even more paper then if the email had been typed and sent on paper as a memo originally.

Chapter 14
Giving Good Discourse

As a corporate employee you will quickly realize that in the corporate world people do not always say what they mean nor do they mean what they say. This can prove especially troublesome to the novice employee who has had little experience in the area of corporate jargon. If you want to be an executive you have to learn to talk like an executive.

Corporate Acronyms

Acronyms were once believed to drastically cut the amount of time necessary to refer to something in speech and written form. In reality, they can be a confusing means of speaking in a type of shorthand that few people understand which gives them a great deal of popularity.

The following are some common acronyms and their translations.

CYA - Cover Your Ass. This is a rather simple, straightforward legal principle that every corporate employee knows quite well. The object is to make sure that whatever happens, you can't be blamed for it.

Memos, correspondence, and the bulk of the volume of inter-office communication is concerned with documenting the fact that certain persons or parties in the office are not responsible for what happened. Thus, it is not a coincidence that "cover your ass" is the motto of most corporate legal departments.

ETA - Estimated Time of Arrival. This acronym was picked up from the military and the airline industry because it sounds more impressive to ask what someone's ETA is rather than when they are expected to show up. The secret to this is to not give your actual estimated time of arrival, but add ten to twenty minutes, depending on how far you have to go.

This approach is rumored to have been made popular by the airlines. For instance, if a plane is scheduled to take off at noon and takes an hour and a half to get to its destination its ETA will be listed as 2:00 PM. The astute among you will quickly note this does not add up.

An extra half hour has been added to the ETA. The plane should actually arrive at 1:30 PM. Adding the extra thirty minutes makes it more likely that it will eventually arrive by its adjusted ETA and thus be 'on time.'

FYI - For Your Information. This is a warning flag on any memo or other form of correspondence you receive. The principle reason of including this on correspondence is to deny the person the correspondence is sent to the excuse of saying they didn't know what the sender was up to.

This makes FYI an immediate signal to you that there may be a great deal of difficulty involved with whatever the correspondence is about.

FYI is a variation of the sleight of hand trick. If someone is sending you something for your information, you can bet what you really need to know isn't in there.

If the memo is too long to read, chances are there is some really damaging news at the very end. This information is put there as whoever sent it is betting you won't read the whole thing. FYI is another way to CYA.

Corporate Jargon

While acronyms give a hint of what they mean, there is a whole body of corporate jargon that bears no resemblance to its meaning. This body of corporate jargon is designed to create subtle metaphors to prevent panic and unwanted rebellions within the corporate ranks.

This means you will have to use words that no one understands including executives. This section is designed as a rough and ready guide to the meanings behind some of the corporate world's most used jargon.

Your proposal is being reviewed. What this actually means is your proposal is sitting on top of the shredder pile. Similarly, your proposal has been reviewed means it has already been shredded.

It goes to committee next month. This really means that your proposal has been lost and hopefully in thirty days you will have forgotten about it.

Frankly, it could go either way. You often get this when you ask someone if they have approved your proposal. What it really means is, "you haven't made it worth my time and effort to approve it yet."

It's going through the process. This actually means that, "we're trying to ignore you, so leave us alone."

It's not presently feasible. You may get this response from your boss when you submit a proposal or suggest a policy revision. What this means is, "it's my idea now."

I'd like to talk about your attitude. When coming from your boss it usually means, "slow down, you're making me look bad."

Would you bring (name of another employee) up to date. This means that (name of another employee) will soon have your job.

I'm concerned about your work. When your boss says this to you, it is best to be prepared to be fired by the end of the month.

I wouldn't worry about it. When you ask a question and an executive replies that he wouldn't worry about it, it's simply because he doesn't have to worry about it. You should.

Restructuring. This is a code word for massive layoffs and budget cuts.

Reassignment. If you are told you are being reassigned it means that you are considered irritating enough for your boss to get rid of you, but you haven't actually done anything to warrant being fired.

We have set up an internal inquiry. "We're sweeping it under the rug."

Promotion. More pay, less responsibility.

Period of Rapid Expansion. This term signifies that the department or company is in a state of chaos and no one really knows what is going on.

Growth period. The company is getting bigger, but making less money.

Seasonal fluctuations. This is often used to explain a lack of revenues, sales, or some other measure of economic success without having to assign any blame to groups or persons within a company. In reality this means the company is losing money and no one knows why.

Unexpected difficulties. This term, like seasonal fluctuations, is an excuse that can be used to avoid apportioning blame within a company. It is a more encompassing phrase and thus useful in a greater number of situations. What it really means more often than not is "we knew this was going to happen, but if we told you, you wouldn't have gone along with the proposal." It can also be used when seasonal fluctuations have been used for too long. (Like for four quarters running.)

We're in the process of renegotiating contracts. This actually means, "we are cutting all benefits and cancelling the healthcare insurance for everyone." (Except for the executives.)

Revenue sharing. "We're going to cut pay rates."

Change in market conditions. This is a convenient excuse for explaining why the budget projections were totally off base.

Cash flow problem. This generally means the corporation can't pay off its debts or collect its accounts receivable. It may also mean a substantial delay before you see your next pay check.

Minor setback. Means there is a grand jury inquiry.

Temporary setback. Lawsuit.

Shakedown period. Nothing is working right.

Hiccup in the market. Bankruptcy is imminent.

Don't call us, we'll call you. They won't call you so you might as well forget about it now.

Chapter 15
I Meet, Therefore I Am

The foundation of all corporate existence is a philosophy that can be encapsulated in the phrase, "I meet, therefore I am." It won't be very long after becoming a corporate employee that you will realize much of your corporate life is going to be taken up by meetings. If you are going to have a successful career as an executive, you will have to learn how to run a meeting.

Meetings serve some useful purposes and even more useless ones. The primary purpose of the meeting seems to be as an excuse for not actually doing any work. Given the time it takes to prepare for meetings, to go to meetings, to meet, and to return from meetings a typical workday can be totally used up.

Corporations like meetings because they are often the only visible sign of activity. You often hear people say, "They must be getting something done, they're meeting all the time." This is a common misconception. When it comes to meetings there is one general rule, the larger the group meeting and the more often it meets, the less that actually gets done. (i.e. Congress.)

The History of The Meeting

The origins of the corporate meeting are shrouded in antiquity. Many experts believe that meetings actually predated the corporation and its predecessor, the limited partnership. It is thought that it was the innate desire of primitive man to meet, create committees, and waste time by just sitting around talking that led to the discovery of the corporation.

Certainly, this is an appealing argument, but we think it will take more meetings, government funding, and a convention in the Caribbean to access the validity of this theory further.

Meetings have changed significantly from their first primitive beginnings. Originally, the force of arms or a simple blow to the head was used to settle disputes during meetings. However, the high turnover in corporate employees due to concussion and death prohibited this practice from continuing.

In ancient Spartan corporations, the side that could shout the loudest prevailed when it came to making decisions at corporate meetings. This method has been adopted extensively in politics. The current means of settling disputes began in ancient Athens. Athenian corporations made decisions democratically by committee, which is likely why they no longer exist.

Over the centuries, a body of rules governing the conduct of the corporate meeting has evolved into a plethora of almost incomprehensible books about the rules of order. You will quickly learn, however, there is one rule they all left out, your boss will do what he damn well pleases, no matter what.

In order to be an executive, you will have to learn how to handle a meeting so that you can manipulate others and advance your position, which is the purpose of meeting in the first place.

First, circulate memos asking people what time they are available to meet. In a time consuming process involving lots of memos and numerous emails (because they take longer to answer than phone calls, which would be simpler), and taking into consideration their various schedules a date is finally set. Finally, a memo is sent out scheduling the meeting for the date and time the most people said they couldn't meet. After all, if they all showed up they might actually do something.

Preparation is key to a successful meeting. When the meeting day arrives preparation is carried out in the morning with the meeting taking place in the early afternoon. After returning from a big lunch most executives will tend to be more sleepy and docile. (If they return at all.)

Don't overlook the most important corporate details like who should or should not sit next to one another, what kind of cookies and punch should be served, and the color of the napkins and tablecloths. You should also consider balloons, streamers, and what kind of alcohol to serve. If you time everything just right you can use up a whole day and get out of work early as well.

The meeting. At the meeting it is customary to review the minutes of the last meeting, set a date for the next meeting, and adjourn. Hopefully, everyone will be so relieved the meeting was not about what they did wrong they won't notice nothing was actually accomplished.

Whatever happens, don't let anyone make a decision. Instead, explore options and discuss them so long that everyone gets tired of hearing about it and forgets why they are there, leaves, or just passes out.

One may think that this is the end of the process, oh no, not yet, there is considerably more 'work' that must be done. After the meeting send out memos stating what you want the official record to say occurred at the meeting. This record usually bears little resemblance to what actually took place other than the time of the meeting, which is why they are called minutes.

The entire meeting process serves merely as a formality to allow executives to make their ideas official company policy. This is why you always want to be the secretary. Nobody in their right mind wants the work of taking minutes, but this is where the real power lies. You can write up the official record the way you want, making you look good and your enemies look bad.

A word of advice, while it may seem glamorous, never 'volunteer' to be the chair. They have no real power and often take the rap for bad decisions that the executives will read about in the 'minutes.' Another word of advice, never miss a meeting for you may come back to find you no longer have a job or worse, no parking space.

Types of Meetings

Departmental planning sessions. The departmental planning meeting is one of the earliest types of meetings to evolve. In hunter gatherer limited partnerships, these meetings were often used to determine what kind of animal to hunt or what should be gathered.

The basic purpose has changed little in the intervening millennia. You will find that your department will have planning sessions during which major departmental tasks are allocated.

In many corporations these departmental planning sessions are held only because it's a tradition rather based on serving any useful purpose. These planning meetings are merely a process of rubber-stamping the predetermined policies of those who control your fate.

Budget meetings. Similar to the departmental planning session, a budget meeting is one at which the expenses of your company are reviewed. Normally, these meetings put the employees under a great deal of scrutiny. It is during these meetings that decisions are made regarding your economic livelihood.

In determining where to spend money and where to cut back, everyone tries to make their department look the best it can. Certainly, the role of your department head is to serve as an advocate for your department because big budgets, large staffs, and increasing expense accounts are all signs of a vibrant and successful department.

Board meetings. Suffice it to say that board meetings rarely bear any real resemblance to the actual actions taken by the board members. These are designed more as a sort of ritualistic formality than any serious attempt to oversee the running of your corporation.

The board meeting is based on an old tribal ritual. The tribal elders, who didn't actually do anything, occasionally got together to drink and reminisce about the good old days of the limited partnership.

In today's corporation, the board of directors meeting is a means by which the corporation can keep the board of directors from bothering the executives. Often times the board of directors are the people who originally started the corporation or their descendants. This ritual keeps these busy bodies out of the way of the 'professional management' who knows how a corporation is supposed to be run.

Personnel review meetings. These are meetings where your supervisors get together and laugh about what you have been up to over the last year, or so. On the surface they are supposed to play a role in determining who will get promoted, who deserves recognition, and who is creating problems within the company. Since this process is shrouded in secrecy you may wonder how recommendations for promotion are actually made.

While practices differ from corporation to corporation, the following are some of the more common methods.
1. Seniority,
2. Promiscuity,
3. Batting average on the softball team, or
4. Random chance.

Disciplinary hearings. Hopefully, you will never have to deal with one of these during your corporate life. Disciplinary hearings are often nerve wracking and troublesome involving a heated exchange of words and possible expulsion from the company.

Depending on what kind of action you are being disciplined for, you will want to try to put as good a face on the situation as possible. Simply calling your accuser a 'bastard' is not likely to persuade the disciplinary committee that you're right. Instead you should appeal to the more basic needs of the committee. Bribes, however, are not a foolproof method of exoneration.

In a disciplinary hearing you are trying to put your best foot forward. The following are some recommended ways to do this.
1. You should arrive on time (especially if you are accused of excessive tardiness),
2. You should be cooperative and agreeable (especially if you are accused of being anti-social and not being a team player), and
3. You should wait your turn to speak and act respectfully (especially if you are accused of insubordination).

The key here is not to reinforce the negative charges that have been brought against you. A disciplinary committee is not going to dismiss the charges against someone they'd just as soon get rid of. You have to give them a reason not to get rid of you.

Some reasons you might try include.
1. You work and play well with others,
2. You still have the photos from the office Christmas party, or
3. You know the Swiss bank account number they're embezzling money into.

Chapter 16
Coffee Breaks
and Time Off For Bad Behavior

As a member of a department clique you will be involved in many kinds of activities with your fellow workers. These activities can include raids on other departments as well as generally wreaking havoc. Despite the exhilaration of conducting day-to-day business, the most time consuming and satisfying activities of your corporate life will be the time you spend not working at all. This chapter's length and detail reflect the importance of these activities, the most important being the coffee break.

Coffee breaks can fall into two distinct types: individual and social. For the individual, a coffee break can be a time of reflection or silent contemplation to restore the soul and help you to face the rest of the workday. Or it can be a time to catch up on personal email and shop online, in other words to not do any work. In a social capacity, it can be an integral part of a complex and intricate socialization ritual. Or simply a time to gossip, in other words to not do any work. Actually they are both pretty much the same thing.

You will cherish the time you spend chatting with your colleagues over coffee creating a feeling of camaraderie within your department. During coffee breaks you will meet and talk with other people who are just like you. You will hear strangely imaginative yarns woven by your fellow workmates as you recount the sights and sounds of the day.

You will soon realize that coffee breaks are an important means of socialization at work (along with meetings). There is something about a coffee break that makes working life seem more palatable. Perhaps because they serve as a time to spread rumors and gossip throughout the department while getting a caffeine buzz.

The History of Coffee Breaks

The origins of the coffee break are thought to predate the existence of coffee itself. While the exact beginning of this tribal practice is lost in the mists of time, it is theorized that it originated not as a 'coffee break' per se, but rather as a 'water break.' While opinions disagree, it is assumed that this practice of allowing employees to drink water during working hours developed out of necessity, rather than ritual.

This theory holds that corporate executives recognized, at an early point, that withholding fluids from employees during working hours led to dehydration, hallucination, and eventually unconsciousness drastically lowering productivity. It was thus an economic necessity to make sure that employees did not lose consciousness, because an unconscious employee is of less use than no employee at all, since they take up valuable office space.

Once this practice was firmly rooted, it took on more ritualistic forms as other beverages were introduced to civilized man. The ancient Egyptians had beer breaks, the Greeks and Romans had wine breaks, the Chinese tea breaks, and the Vikings had mead breaks while they weren't plundering the civilized world.

The modern coffee break has its roots steeped in tradition and legend. Some scholars believe coffee was first discovered in the 9th century, while other scholars disagree, not for any particular reason, but because they are angling for a grant.

Coffee is thought to have been discovered by an Ethiopian goat herder who noticed that when his goats ate the berries from a particular bush they acted peculiar. The goats had more energy, didn't need sleep, and started gossiping. So, he did the sensible thing, he ate the berries himself and the coffee bean was discovered.

In the 15th century coffee was brought from Arabia to Abyssinia and Yemen because of its ability to dissipate drowsiness and prevent sleep during long corporate meetings and religious services. Coffee hadn't yet spread to the rest of the world so, in order to go out for a coffee break, you had a very long journey which may account for its lack of popularity at the time.

By the 16th century the coffee break had reached Constantinople. However, coffee breaks were seen to be reducing productivity and impeding religious observances, so they were banned in Mecca. Later, coffee was banned in Turkey and Ethiopia because it was associated with political rabble, which made it even more popular.

The first coffeehouse opened in Britain in 1652 and it wasn't long before coffeehouses became places where people gathered to complain about the government. This tension was compounded by the Great London Fire of 1666, which was blamed on political rabble, although it is now thought to have started in a bake house in Pudding Lane by employees trying to roast coffee beans. (While warming up their lunch.)

So, in 1675 King Charles II tried to ban coffee breaks branding those who partook of them as rabble-rousers who were disturbing the peace. The ban failed and the coffee break soon became a time for people to share the news of the day, criticize their leaders, and generally waste time. This provided an early model for the modern corporate coffee break and was likely why governments tried to ban them.

Corporations were forced to officially adopt the coffee break in the workplace because their employees would otherwise have to go out of the building to a coffeehouse for coffee significantly reducing the likelihood of their returning to work. Nowadays, coffee breaks keep employees in the building and closer to their desk, so companies can get more work out of them. It also makes it less likely for employees to engage in political rabble in a coffeehouse.

Coffee and The Corporation

Coffee has a long and remarkable corporate history. Coffee has more significance to your company than just being something acceptable to drink to get a buzz at work. Coffee and the companies who first brought it to the west had a direct influence on how corporations work and how the people who run them, like your CEO, behave.

The first multinational corporation to issue stock to the public was the Dutch East India Company. Founded in 1602, it imported coffee to Europe on a large scale from Ceylon (i.e. Sri Lanka) and Java in Indonesia. It held a virtual monopoly on many imported goods like sugar, spices, cotton, and silk from the Far East. By 1669 it was the wealthiest corporation the world had ever seen (up until then).

It had the power to coin money, negotiate treaties, establish colonies, raise an army, and wage war. It was the dream of every corporate executive come true. It had all the powers of government, except unlike government, it provided things people actually wanted, and it made a profit.

However, like government over the next 100 (or so) years the increasing costs of maintaining an army and waging war, coupled with a decline in trade and a drop in prices wreaked financial havoc. Competition from cheap imports and a fierce price war with the British, and a few real wars with them as well, slashed profits. Increasing overhead, corruption, and more competition from cheap imports led to increasing deficits and a growing debt. So in 1800 the Dutch East India Company went bankrupt and was officially dissolved.

Correspondingly, the British had analogous corporate machinations, which ironically resulted a similar fate. (i.e. they had the same idea and went bust too.) In 1588 a group of London merchants petitioned Queen Elizabeth to sail to the Indian Ocean. So, in 1600 they formed the British East India Company, which also traded with the East Indies. It traded in coffee, tea, cotton, silk, indigo dye, salt, and opium (yes, opium).

The British East India Company grew rich and powerful eventually ruling most of the Indian subcontinent. Like the Dutch, it too had the right to mint money, acquire territory, make alliances with other governments, command troops, execute criminals (or rebellious employees), and make war. It was every CEO's dream come true.

However, there was a drop in the market and a recession in Europe so the British were forced to turn to the government for a bailout. (Sounds familiar.) In response, the Tea Act of 1773 was passed which had other ramifications. It gave the British Company an exemption from taxes others had to pay. As a result, American merchants had to pay more taxes while competing with cheap foreign imports.

This created unrest in the American colonies that led to the Boston Tea Party and American Revolution, which contrary to popular opinion, was really about coffee and the right to have coffee breaks.

Ironically, when coffee was first introduced to the American colonies, it was not successful because these early Americans preferred drinking alcohol.

Eventually, the British Parliament passed economic and military reforms taking control of the Company and its India territory while nationalizing its armies. Overwhelmed by a growing debt imposed by increased government regulation, the British East India Company went bankrupt and was officially dissolved in 1874.

These early attempts at creating a stockholder owned multinational corporation set the pace for the many corporations that would soon follow. It shows that a business grows and prospers by providing useful things that people want and when they get involved in government and politics, it leads to their demise. A tradition that carries on to this day.

Types of Coffee

Think your coffee tastes like crap? Maybe it does because that's where some coffee comes from.

It all started back in the 18th century. The Dutch established coffee plantations in the Dutch East Indies planting Arabica coffee from Yemen.

During this time local farmers were prohibited from taking any coffee beans for their own use, but they still wanted a cup of coffee. They noticed that the Asian Palm Civet, a weasel-like mammal ate coffee berries for the fruit which covers the seed and the undigested coffee beans were left in their droppings.

So they gathered the beans, cleaned and roasted them. They discovered that the coffee beans had fermented in the animal's stomach reducing its acidity making a mild cup of coffee. Since then coffee made from these beans found in droppings has become highly prized and very expensive.

Today it has affectionately become known as poo coffee. If you think your job stinks try picking coffee beans out of a pile of poo every day. It's bad enough picking them up when they fall on the floor.

Once the crap coffee craze caught on, almost anything with poo would do. In Brazil the Jacu bird eats coffee beans and excretes them in their droppings. Elephants in Thailand eat Arabica coffee beans and excrete them into huge piles of dung that have to be gone through by hand to extract the beans.

Poo coffee can sell for between $200 and $600 a pound! Mostly because it takes that much money to get people to go in there after them. So, you too might be able to make a fortune if you can get your pet pachyderm, bird, or cat to eat coffee beans.

Coffee and Caffeine

Coffee breaks became popular because coffee has many useful side effects. Coffee became the break of choice in the modern corporate world because it falls into a medicinal class of food that has a stimulant effect upon the central nervous system. It can increase employee endurance while reducing fatigue creating a feeling of exhilaration that replicates the effects of mild alcohol intoxication, which is why it became popular in the workplace.

A word of caution, use of coffee can lead to feelings of excitement, alertness, clarity, and actually getting something done. In spite what you may have heard drinking coffee will not make you happier, smarter, or better looking. That's what alcohol is for.

Now let's get to the real purpose of the coffee break, getting a caffeine buzz. Caffeine commonly consumed by humans comes from the seed of the coffee plant, the leaves of the tea bush, and the kola nut. Recreational caffeine use increases alertness and wards off drowsiness that can lead to improved physical and cognitive functions. However, caffeine can be a gateway drug leading to other substance abuse including espresso, cappuccino, and even demitasse.

Caffeine abuse can lead to a more serious condition known as caffeine intoxication. Symptoms can include anxiety, insomnia, increased urination, rambling speech, irritability, lapses in judgment, disorientation, loss of inhibitions, or delusions of grandeur. Which may (or may not) explain your coworkers' behavior.

Treatment of severe caffeine intoxication usually involves treatment of the immediate symptoms, but if the patient has high serum levels of caffeine then dialysis or blood filtration may be required. Caffeine withdrawal is categorized as a medical disorder and withdrawal can last up to 9 days. So, if you play your cards right, you can apply for a medical leave and get some paid time off to boot.

Tea Breaks

In some parts of the world, coffee is not the generally accepted break of choice. The 17th century saw the beginning of one of the greatest splits within established sacred rituals the world has ever seen. It was earth shattering and affects all of us to this day. It happened on the grounds of differences in deeply held belief and practice, leading to the setting up of separate corporate traditions. No, it wasn't the Great Papal Schism of 1378 with the two rival Popes of Rome and Avignon, France. This was the Great Coffee and Tea Schism.

Around 1660, Catherine, the wife of King Charles II (the guy who tried to ban coffee), tried to introduce tea breaks to England because she liked tea. The British introduced tea cultivation to India to break the Chinese monopoly on it. However, it would take until the 18th century for it to really catch on.

The Dutch controlled most of the world's coffee production, so the British attempted growing coffee in Ceylon. Natural disasters wiped out these coffee plantations, leaving British corporations at the mercy of the Dutch monopoly. Employees of British companies grew restless as the supply of coffee for coffee breaks dwindled.

In an effort to maintain law and order the British corporate community resorted to the use of tea instead of coffee as a source of caffeine. So began the tea break, which has become a British institution. This Great Schism between coffee and tea persists into modern times.

Tea was thought to have been discovered in ancient times when leaves accidentally fell into boiling water making an aromatic drink. It became widely popular by the 10th century during the Tang Dynasty. Ironically, there wasn't a popular beverage named Tang until the 20th century. Tea was used in China for medicinal as well as pleasurable purposes, much like alcohol is used in other parts of the world.

Throughout history many cultures have elevated serving tea to an art form in order to make an everyday activity more entertaining for culture reasons, but mostly because television hadn't been invented yet. The drinking of tea has led to many social rituals such as the tea ceremony, tea dances, tea party, tea garden, tea rose, and becoming teed off. Drinking tea can be the high point of social gatherings because of its ability to hide just about any kind of alcohol.

How To Have Coffee Breaks

Coffee can be prepared in virtually an unlimited number of ways. Some of the most popular include; a pot of boiling water, mixed with an egg, a percolator, drip, espresso, cappuccino, and French press. There are an unlimited number of varieties of beans, methods to roast them, and means to grind them. There are a myriad of flavorings, spices, and sweeteners that can be added to coffee. This means that what kind of coffee your department has on its breaks could very likely be the most difficult and divisive decision it will ever face.

No endeavor is ever complete without having the right gear. To have a successful coffee break one must be properly equipped. Coffee gear includes the right coffee maker, grinder, storage container, serving tray, water kettle, spoon, sugar bowl, cream pitcher, cup, and saucer or mug. Or just a Styrofoam cup.

More than any other personal possession the coffee mug is an expression of an employee's individuality. While it is acceptable for personal taste to dictate the appearance of the coffee mug, certain overriding concerns come into play.
1. Coffee mugs should be coffee tight (they should not leak).
2. Coffee mugs should be washed out at least once a week (or every 100 cups).
3. Despite the individualistic nature of the coffee mug, anti-corporate slogans like "People Before Profits" and "Corporate Responsibility," are generally considered in poor taste.

An important question that has perplexed bosses everywhere is how frequently should their employees have a coffee break. The frequency and duration of each employee's coffee break can be a tough decision for their boss. A few things to consider are how many months the employee has been employed, their size, and their attentiveness.

When it comes to giving employees coffee it's important to be patient with them, especially the newly hired as it may take some time for them to settle down to a regular schedule of coffee breaks. Having a schedule works well if an employee does not mind being woken up every two hours for a coffee break

There are some bosses who leave a great deal of autonomy in the hands of their employees to decide when to take their coffee breaks. Not having a strict schedule works well if an employee is prone to sleepiness or is relatively docile. However, having employees determine when to have their own coffee breaks can result in no work getting done at all.

You may have a new employee who does not finish all of his coffee during a break. Avoid the inclination to use guilt to get him to finish his coffee. Telling him that there are corporate employees in Africa who don't have coffee can make him upset and cranky (even more than normal). It might even provoke him to turn to tea breaks, which is the slippery slope to a public sector job.

Lunch Breaks

In the middle of each workday you will have an extended coffee break called your lunch hour. The lunch hour is basically a more advanced version of a coffee break involving the consumption of not only liquids, but solids on a larger scale than a coffee break.

You may well ask when should a new employee start taking lunch. There is no established time when an employee should begin having lunch. For the first couple of months an employee generally gets everything he needs from coffee breaks. The first solid lunch is usually introduced several months after employment. Employees who are not used to solid food for lunch may be more comfortable starting out with coffee then gradually adding something more solid to eat.

While the term lunch hour, by its very name, designates a fixed amount of time for lunch, not all lunch hours are 60 minutes in duration. For some employees a lunch hour may consist of only 30 minutes, whereas for others it may stretch well into the afternoon. Generally, the length of your 'lunch hour' depends on what capacity you are employed. Corporate executives, for example, may have what would be more appropriately deemed 'lunch afternoons.'

There are several tried and true means of having lunch during the workday.
1. Brown bagging,
2. Employee lunchroom,
3. Cafeteria, and
4. Restaurants.

1. Brown bag. The brown bag lunch is the oldest and most traditional form of lunch. Sadly, it has fallen into ill repute as greater affluence has made other types of lunch more popular. While it is referred to as a brown bag lunch, the brown bag refers to the container in which the lunch is kept in, not the lunch itself.

Despite its name, a brown bag lunch can be brought to work in any sort of container. The key is that it is a lunch brought from home to work, not one purchased from another source nor one provided at the place of employment. However, it can be appropriated from a fellow coworker during a coffee break.

After much analysis, it seems that the stigma that now surrounds the brown bag lunch derives not so much from the container, but from the contents. To put it simply, brown bag lunches have had a tendency to consist of suspect culinary material. People bringing delicacies such as poached sea urchin to work have resulted in the terrorizing of coworkers with threats like, "But there's enough for everyone."

This brings us to the rules that govern brown bag lunches.
1. No one else wants to know what you're having for lunch,
2. Keep your lunch to yourself, and
3. Do not bring 'enough for everyone.'

While they still carry a stigma, tremendous improvements have been made in the area of brown bag lunches. It goes without saying that lunches brought from home predate the existence of brown bags and lunch boxes. Before brown bags cloth sacks, wooden boxes, and vessels made of clay were all used to bring food to work.

All of these methods are considered to be greatly superior to the original practice of bringing dead animals to work, or even live animals, for preparation over an open fire in the office. To complicate the reputation of brown bag lunches even further, some scholars now believe that Pandora's Box was actually an employee's lunch box left out in the sun too long.

2. Employee lunchroom. The employee lunchroom was designed to separate those people prone to wanting to share their lunch with their coworkers from the rest of the office. Employee lunchrooms discourage employees from eating their lunches at their desks where they can easily antagonize nearby coworkers.

The first rule in establishing employee lunchrooms is to make sure they are downwind of the rest of the corporate offices. Employee lunch rooms now incorporate a great deal of highly advanced technological support systems to augment employee lunches like vending machines and microwave ovens.

Vending machines. These insidious devices have permeated all of society. The primary purpose of these machines is to relieve you of whatever cash you have in your pocket. They provide you with a wide variety of interesting comestibles, all of which have a shelf life longer than your lifetime.

Microwave ovens. These have become a constant source of employee amusement. Originally designed to provide a fast means of heating entrees purchased in vending machines, other uses were quickly found for these devices.

Putting metal objects in the microwave to make 'fireworks' and turning normal potatoes into explosive devices have now become popular, but dangerous pastimes.

3. Cafeteria. Partially in response to the backlash against brown bag lunches, companies began providing cafeterias where their employees could purchase their lunch. Some companies found it necessary to provide provisions for their employees since circumstances would prohibit the employees providing their own food. The prefabrication of strange and unrecognizable types of what some like to call 'food' has given cafeterias a stigma that equals, if not exceeds, the brown bag lunch.

The cafeteria was first implemented on a large scale during the time of the Roman Empire. The Romans had large ships called galleys that were propelled by oars or sails. Sailing personnel onboard Roman galleys were fed via a central trough where food was deposited to slide down to each employee. This enabled employees to keep working at their desk, so they could continue rowing while they ate so the ship would keep moving.

This method of serving food in a company cafeteria was adopted by the modern corporation not so much as a benefit to their employees, but as a ploy to keep workers as close to their work as possible to keep the corporate ship moving. Which is why a cafeteria's kitchen is often called a galley.

Further enhancing the mystique of corporate lunches was the use of mystery meat, which was invented to feed Napoleon's troops as they retreated from Moscow in 1812. While the substance actually used in mystery meat has improved, somewhat, from the original source used by Napoleon's catering staff, its introduction to corporate cuisine is heralded as ushering in the era of unrecognizable food. This innovation proved so popular it spread to schools, hospitals, and cafeterias everywhere.

Employee lunchrooms and cafeterias are not to be confused with the executive dining room. (They never are.) The origin of the executive dining room was not to serve food, per se, but to establish a place where executives could be separate from the ordinary rabble. The primary difference between the two is, well, everything.

4. Restaurants. Eating out was a concept developed early in the development of the corporate world. History is full of myth and legend surrounding corporate employees going out to eat.

Before restaurants existed, groups of corporate employees would often go to the nearest town or country in search of something to eat. Historians have often mistaken these large scale corporate lunches for invasions.

In one such instance, a large scale corporate lunch by the Huns and their CEO Attila was misconstrued as an invasion by the emperor of the Western Roman Empire. In reaction to this 'invasion,' an army comprised of Imperial troops and Visigoths attacked and defeated the Huns at Chalons, France, in 451 A. D.

The Huns subsequently decided to try Italian, rather than French food. The death of Attila in 453 A. D. resulted in the Huns fixing something at home, and no longer going out for lunch.

The development and diversification of restaurants enabled hungry employees to go out for a specific type of food (e.g. French, Italian, Chinese, etc.) without actually having to go to that country. This development can be construed as directly responsible for a corresponding drop in what has been described as roving nomadic tribes and invading hordes of marauding barbarians, which were more often than not simply a large number of corporate employees out looking for something for lunch.

While current restaurant lunches rarely results in armed conflict, they can be just as deadly to your career as if the participants were armed. Today, power lunches have harkened back to the days of roving bands of corporate employees pillaging towns and terrorizing the countryside.

You may well ask how do you survive under these grueling circumstances. Proper etiquette and conduct is essential in these situations. While there is a great deal of leeway in deciding what you want to eat for a power lunch, there is one overriding rule. Do not order quiche! Similarly, you should avoid any signs of weakness, fear, or intimidation during these lunches.

Below are some of the more popular trials of strength and endurance during these lunches.
1. Seeing who can hold their hand over the open candle flame the longest,
2. Seeing who can belch the loudest,
3. Seeing who can spit the farthest,
4. Seeing who can stuff the most grapes in their mouth at one time, and
5. Seeing who can urinate the farthest with the greatest accuracy (while this should be for men only and only in the rest room, in today's corporate culture of equality this is not always the case.)

Time Off

Personal Errands. Sooner or later it will become necessary for you to take time off of work for personal emergencies. (In other words skipping out of work.) The following passage is designed to help you deal with this eventuality.

There are basically three methods you can try to get out of the office for a personal errand.
1. Ask permission from your boss,
2. Sneak out, or
3. Create a diversion.

After the first method fails, you will have to resort to one of the other two methods of trying to get out of the office. Trying to sneak out is the most often used, but least successful method. The primary problem in this method is that most people aren't very good at sneaking out of the office.

The first and most often transgressed rule is that you are not supposed to tell anyone you are sneaking out. You should also avoid using closely guarded exits. Windows are a good means of escaping, but only if your office is just a few floors above the ground. Wearing some sort of disguise or camouflage will help.

The choice of disguise is important because you want to be inconspicuous, so avoid the following.
1. Clown costumes of any type,
2. Period dress (no Robin Hood, it's a dead giveaway), or
3. Costumes that make you look like your boss.

Remember, while a filing cabinet may work well as camouflage, if it is moving around the office it is bound to attract attention.

Due to the problems involved in sneaking out of the office the third option becomes the most useful. In creating a diversion you divert attention from yourself and hopefully sneak out in the ensuing confusion.

The following are some diversions, although they are not recommended.
1. Set a wastepaper basket on fire,
2. Set off the sprinkler system,
3. Hide the coffee for the coffee machine,
4. Scream "corporate takeover!" at the top of your lungs, or
5. Lock an executive in the restroom.

If the personal errand is early in the day or of short duration, you will find it necessary to get back into your office. This can prove more difficult than actually getting out of the office. While you may have escaped detection getting out, people will likely notice you sneaking in, as this rarely occurs. If all else fails, just forget trying to get back to work and take the afternoon off.

Leaving work early. For various and sundry reasons you may wish to leave your office before you are supposed to. You can use any of the methods listed under the heading personal errands to attempt to leave your place of work early. The difference between leaving work early and going out on a personal errand is that you don't have to sneak back into the office once you have gotten out.

If you are caught outside of the office by a fellow employee during office hours try the following excuses.

1. Pretend you lost your memory,
2. Pretend you were sleep walking,
3. Tell them you were kidnapped by corporate raiders, or
4. Tell them you are spying on them and if they pay you, you won't report them to their boss.

You will also want to avoid your absence being noticed by anyone in the office. In order to make people think you are hard at work you should,

1. Leave a light on in the window,
2. Turn a radio or television on,
3. Have your mail held at the post office, and
4. Cancel all newspaper and magazine subscriptions until you get back.

Arriving late. Almost certainly you will be in the position of arriving late for work. The best way to deal with this is to try to get into your office without being noticed. While there are many techniques to do this, the most effective seems to be pretending you are a corporate executive.

If this fails you may have to explain the reason for your arriving late at the office. Unfortunately, honesty is not always the best policy under these circumstances.

The following are a few guidelines for excuses.

1. Never give an excuse that can be verified (especially if it is not true),
2. Mentioning contagious diseases usually results in less questioning by your supervisors, and
3. Never tell them you were looking for another job.

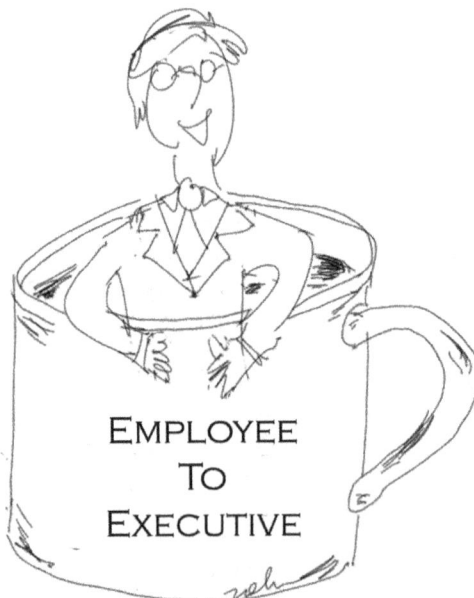

EMPLOYEE
TO
EXECUTIVE

Chapter 17
Corporate Life and Death

Each and every corporation and department (maybe not every) has to come from somewhere. So you might ask, where do corporations come from? Well, this can be an embarrassing question for some executives. They might say something like, the CEO found your corporation in a field or it fell out of the sky.

In reality, when a couple of entrepreneurs care about commerce very much and want to make a corporate way of life together they will often incorporate and soon they will have a brand spanking new company they can love forever.

Some corporations are created by limited partners who may be young and in-experienced. They might realize that they cannot provide their new corporation with everything it might need. So they make the difficult decision to have it adopted by a more mature corporation that can better attend to its needs.

Some corporations come from limited partnerships that broke up and went their separate ways. These partners may form partnerships with other partners and create their own corporations. This can cause their employees to become confused making them act out or rebel against the corporate way of life. They may even runaway and join the government.

Some limited partnerships can stay together for years while other executives in-corporate around with many partners making lots of little companies. When a limited partnership breaks up it can be difficult for all the employees involved.

Employees from broken companies can have a tendency to be disruptive to the smooth running of the corporation doing things like starting a recycling program or a profit sharing plan. They may act out because they feel it was their fault the partners split up.

When one CEO who already has his own company meets another and they hit it off, they may decide to merge their companies. If they take the big step to merge, it can be a very trying time in your corporate life. While they may say they are equals, one partner will usually end up on top.

There will be lots of new people to meet, which means you will have to learn a lot of new names. However, if it was your company that took over the other company don't worry about learning any names, most of these new people will be gone by Christmas. Nevertheless, if the merger goes bad it is all too often the employees who suffer.

For those who are not chased away, literally, feelings of jealousy and rivalry about the new company are to be expected. To help ease these feelings, a boss should tell his employees beforehand that a merger is on the way and its due date to make the disruption of a merger as small as possible.

There will come a time when the executives will have to decide where to have their office. They can't keep two office locations for very long and they will want to office together. If there are a lot of employees you may find yourself having to share your office with a new coworker. Or worse, you may be uprooted and have to move all your stuff into an unfamiliar place and live with people you have never met before. This might make an employee runaway, but most of the time they are eventually found huddled in their old, empty office.

A merger can disturb the regular patterns of everyday office life. Everyone is bound to feel fatigued and frustrated due to the stress of the merger. They may not display these feelings until some small incident arises, like the new arrivals borrowing their office equipment or getting a budget increase, making them lose their temper. Your boss may want to encourage the older employees to share some of their office equipment that is outdated or no longer works with the new arrivals to help develop a sense of generosity.

There are three basic outcomes when two corporations merge.
1. The integrating of both cultures. The raiders stay, marry local women, and have children. (Not necessarily in that order.)
2. The creation of a new culture that contains elements of both, in other words, no one gets their way, or
3. The continuance of both cultures creating a perpetual war where both fight for total dominance.

Then there is the brand new acquisition. There may come a time when you find out that your corporation has acquired a brand spanking new company. When this happens, the older employees may feel jealous because their executives are paying more attention to the new acquisition instead of them. As a result, the older employees may want to gain attention by relapsing into old patterns and even act as if they are a new acquisition themselves.

The older employees may be reluctant to accept the new acquisition. They may want to return the new employees to the other company. Some employees may not demonstrate a sense of jealousy or rivalry immediately. They may say how wonderful the new acquisition is then one day abruptly say, "now we can get rid of it." Employees may even feel hostile towards their own executives who made this acquisition.

This jealousy can manifest itself in several ways.
1. Employees amble about the office aimlessly (more so than normal),
2. Employees seem to have lost all interest in things that once preoccupied them (e.g. sports, gossip, coffee breaks), or
3. There is an increased incident of 'accidents' in the office.

Executives may try to force their older employees into accepting the new acquisition, but this usually doesn't work very well. They may misbehave even more than normal by pulling pranks on the new acquisition like putting their hand in warm water when they are napping, then tipping over the water cooler and blaming the 'accident' on the new acquisition.

There are a few things executives can do to help alleviate this tension.
1. Protect the new acquisition from the older employees by locking them in the broom closet,
2. Tell the older employees that any pranks against the new acquisition will not be tolerated, even if they are really funny, and
3. Make the older employees understand that their executives still love them very much, (but not too much).

If your company has merged with another company, your company may have been quietly taken over. Nowadays it common for takeovers to happen behind the scenes. Due to potential negative ramifications, a merger may actually be a hostile takeover in disguise, and sometimes it's a really good disguise.

If you are not sure, here's a way to tell. Merged companies often have weird hyphenated names, like married couples, which includes the names of both parties. So, the company name that comes first is the one who has taken over the other one.

Here's how to tell if your company has quietly been taken over hostilely.
1. If the name of your company has been chiseled off the building and another name is there.
2. If your 'new' boss tells you to do things his company's (new) way or hit the highway.
3. If your office is full of new faces and you can't find the guy who had the desk next to you last week.
4. If your CEO, executives, or offices have moved to another city, state, or country.
5. If all your personal belongings are on the sidewalk outside the building.

The Corporate Takeover

Sooner or later in your corporate life chances are you will come face to face with the possibility of a corporate takeover. While the corporate takeover has gotten much publicity of late, it is as old as the corporation itself.

The first corporate takeovers were primarily military in nature. Corporate conflicts were determined by who had the most guns (or swords, spears, arrows, etc.). Rival corporate employees were simply shot (or before the invention of gunpowder they were stabbed, bludgeoned, garroted, hung, or disemboweled), and the corporate offices were burned.

The annals of history are filled with corporate rivalries and takeovers. Perhaps the most famous corporate takeover occurred in the 17th century. The Dutch East India Company was granted a monopoly to trade with Africa and the East Indies. In 1600, Queen Elizabeth chartered the British East India Company giving it a trade monopoly from the Cape of Good Hope in South Africa and east to the Straits of Magellan in South America.

The Dutch East India Company became the market leader with branch offices throughout the East Indies and Africa. In order to improve their market share and takeover control of the areas dominated by the Dutch East India Company, the British East India Company had the corporate employees of the Dutch East India Company shot and their corporate offices burnt.

Eventually, both the British East India Company and the Dutch East India Company went bankrupt which should be a lesson to all corporations and executives who may wish to engage in this type of unscrupulous behavior. Don't go bankrupt.

In today's modern world, corporate raiders have been forced to resort to ever more brutal and vicious means of taking over rival corporations. These can include website postings, hackers, social media campaigns, and other ferocious online attacks. Rumor, gossip, and governmental investigations can escalate the attack. If these tactics don't work, they may have to resort to generous stock offers and executive buyout packages. All these methods have made the corporate takeover more perilous than ever.

While the physical torture of the employees of corporations that have been taken over has been prohibited, it has been replaced by far more sinister and hideous means of breaking an employee's spirit such as sensitivity training, teambuilding workshops, and self-improvement seminars.

You might wonder what you and your department should to do in case of a corporate takeover. Your actions as a corporate employee depend on what kind of takeover is being attempted. In the case of a friendly takeover the board of directors has sold out your company for a very handsome profit, so your duty is to face the consequences of their actions. On the other hand, a hostile takeover is to be fought to the last employee or until a higher price is offered. And despite what he says, it is customary for the chief executive officer to go down with his corporation.

At the first sign of hostile takeover, you as a corporate employee should take part in organized resistance against the invaders. Your fellow workers will mobilize all their resources in an effort to discourage the threatened takeover. There are several means that corporations can employ to discourage a hostile takeover.

The first line of defense in preventing a corporate takeover is known as the Possum defense. Like the marsupial it is named after, your company attempts to play dead to discourage the predator corporation from eating it alive.

This defense requires all employees to do the following;
1. Turn out all the lights,
2. Don't answer the door or the phones,
3. Pretend there is no one in the office, and
4. Be very, very quiet.

With any luck, the corporate raider will assume that the corporation no longer exists and will move on to more lively corporations.

The second line of defense in preventing a corporate takeover is known as the Skunk defense. This is a self-damaging and deprecating defense used to make your company distasteful to the predator corporation trying to take it over.

This defense suggests the following tactics.
1. Leak stories to the predator corporation about your company supporting left wing liberal causes,
2. Leak stories to the predator corporation about your company supporting right wing conservative political candidates,
3. Leak stories to the predator corporation about key company executives being former political appointees, or
4. Paint a white stripe on the building.

With any luck, this will make your company stink so badly that any self-respecting corporate raider will want to distance himself as far as possible from it.

The third line of defense in preventing a corporate takeover is known as the Blowfish defense. This defense designed to choke the predator corporation by keeping it as busy as possible to prevent it from swallowing your company.

The tropical ocean fish this defense is named after suggests using these tactics.
1. Send as much useless junk mail as possible to the predator corporation to keep its secretarial staff so busy that they cannot get any real work done,
2. Call the predator corporation and hang up (repeat frequently),
3. Anonymously send the executives of the predator corporation hundreds of 'secret' documents for their review, and
4. Go to the offices of the predator corporation's chief executive officer, key corporate executives, and board of directors; ring doorbell and run away (repeat as often as necessary).

Although making your company appear larger, even poisonous, like the tropical Blowfish, some corporations can still be eaten by predators after special preparation.

The fourth line of defense in preventing a corporate takeover is known as the Sloth defense. Like the South American arboreal creature it is named after, this defense dictates making your company look as slow as possible. (Warning, in some corporations this 'go slow' approach might not even be noticed.)

As a corporate employee, you should,
1. Lower productivity as much as possible (for some departments further reductions in productivity may be extremely difficult),
2. Take longer lunches,
3. Leave early, and
4. Come to work late.

The fifth line of defense in preventing a corporate takeover is known as the Chameleon defense. The purpose of this defense is to be as difficult to find as possible.

It dictates the following strategy.
1. Change the location of your company offices as often as possible (be sure to tell all employees where the new office is located),
2. Change your company's name as often as possible (which may result in a drop in corporate name recognition),
3. All company phone numbers should be unpublished (which may result in a significant drop in sales), and
4. If anyone asks you, deny all knowledge of your company.

This policy is most effective when implemented before the threat of a corporate takeover becomes apparent. Once they have located your company this defense loses much of its effectiveness.

These are just a few of the most commonly used means to fight a corporate takeover, but innovation is constantly occurring in the area of corporate takeover defenses. If all else fails, try offering some lower level employees as sort of a sacrifice to placate the hunger of the raiding corporation.

In case of occupation. Despite the best efforts of your company to fight to the last employee, corporate takeovers do occur. If this happens to your company you will feel the thrill of being part of the exciting resistance, a freedom fighter, a saboteur within the corporate hierarchy fighting behind the lines for the corporate way of life. Your departmental call will be your battle cry and your corporate logo will be your battle standard.

Your duty to your department is to make life as difficult as possible for the occupying corporation. Acts of internal sabotage such as jamming copy machines and plugging the toilets can bring the occupying corporation to its knees.

In acts of sabotage let your creativity shine through. Lots of interesting things can be accomplished with data damaging computer viruses, a little tinkering with the telephone system, flushing important documents down the toilet, and a whole host of other activities.

Hopefully, a sustained, well executed reign of terror will force the occupying corporation to withdraw its stock offer and retreat, leaving you and your company intact.

Nothing stays the same and the same is true for corporations. While we all want them to go on forever, the reality is many corporations dwindle away for years to nothing without anyone even noticing, and then their name is bought by a Korean conglomerate. Others go out in a blaze of glory leading to criminal investigations.

Signs that your company is dwindling.
1. Executives are now using the regular employees' washroom.
2. Regular employees are using the washroom at the gas station.
3. There are less people at the office party.
4. There are less office parties.
5. There is less actual office.

Has anyone besides you come to work lately? Have you received a paycheck recently? If you answered no to either of these questions the company you have been working for may actually no longer exist.

Other warning signs are as follows.
1. You have not received any memos recently.
2. No one has asked to borrow money from you at work of late.
3. The utilities at the corporate offices have been disconnected.
4. Your key to the office no longer fits the locks.
5. There haven't been any meetings lately.

While death rarely occurs for departments in large corporations it is relatively common among small companies. Bureaucracies being what they are the higher-ups may actually forget to notify some of the employees affected. There are many stories of branch offices continuing to function even though the main corporation had gone bankrupt decades earlier.

This allegedly happened after World War II when there were rumors of Japanese branch offices in the Pacific continuing operations long after the parent corporation ceased to exist simply due to lack of proper notice.

If you suspect that your department or company no longer exists, this can be an opportunity to furnish your home with worn out furniture or get that outmoded, obsolete fax machine you always wanted to buy ten years ago, but couldn't afford. If no one cares about your department any longer, they may no longer care about its furniture and office equipment providing you with many mementos.

Chapter 18
Elevator Etiquette
Getting Off On The Right Floor

As buildings get taller the time employees spend in elevators gets longer. In some jobs you can spend most of your working life in elevators, if you're lucky. Sadly, too many times elevators have been the scene of breaches in proper etiquette and civilized behavior.

In order to reestablish proper etiquette in the corporate world, this chapter lays out the official rules of elevator use. Since so much time is spent by corporate employees in the elevator, the utmost should be done to make it a pleasurable experience. Knowing the official rules of elevator use can help reestablish proper elevator etiquette.

Stairways and Stairwells. No discussion of elevator etiquette would be complete without first dealing with the alternative to the elevator, the stairway. Shy and retiring or just plain anti-social people may find this chapter on elevator etiquette too intense and intrusive.

If you do not want to take part in proper elevator etiquette we suggest you use the stairs, after all that's what they are there for. In time these anti-social types, especially those who work in very tall buildings will come to appreciate the pleasurable experience of a proper elevator ride.

Entering the elevator. First and foremost, the most important rule in entering an elevator is that you wait for anyone who is getting off. It is only polite to wait for everyone who wishes to, to exit the elevator before you attempt to enter it. Simultaneous embarking and disembarking is not only improper, it's potentially hazardous to life and limb. Violation of this basic rule can result in suspension and even banishment from the elevator.

The exception to this rule is if several of your friends are getting on and someone you don't like from a rival department is trying to get off. In this case, you rush your opponent preventing them from getting off the elevator. Then you can while the time away seeing how long you can keep them from getting off. You can have fun ejecting them on the wrong floor like the sub-sub-basement or the CEO's floor.

Greeting new entrants. The current state of affairs in greeting new entrants to the elevator is in great disrepair. New entrants are acknowledged only when they are previously known to one of the current residents of the elevator, otherwise they go totally ignored. Staring at the lights displaying what floor you are on is not only silly, it's rude and potentially hazardous.

The residents of the elevator should establish a welcoming committee as they enter the elevator on the top or bottom floors of the trip depending on which direction the elevator is heading. Traditionally, the person going to the highest floor, or conversely the lowest floor if the elevator is going down is the de facto chairman of the welcoming committee.

However, this is more tradition than necessity. You should elect a committee chair and establish bylaws by the time you get to the second or third floor. Whatever bylaws you wish to use to establish the chairmanship of the committee is acceptable if the residents of the elevator agree by a simple majority vote.

Upon creation of the committee, and appointment of the chairman, all new entrants into the elevator are to be greeted by a cheery hello, good morning, good afternoon, or whatever the circumstances dictate, introduced to the other residents of the elevator, and wished a pleasant and enjoyable elevator ride.

As you travel up or down new inhabitants of the elevator should be welcomed and introduced to the group in order to make them feel at home and make their ride as enjoyable as possible.

If for any reason the chairman of the welcoming committee is not seen as living up to his duties a two-thirds vote of the residents of the elevator may impeach that chairman from his position. In extreme cases, expulsion from the elevator can be enforced at the next stop. Similarly, any person not doing their most to make the elevator ride enjoyable for the rest of their traveling companions can be expelled at the next stop.

Food. Offering cookies, cakes, lemonade, coffee, etc. while not required is encouraged, based upon availability, to greet new entrants. Fresh baked cookies are a homey touch. A picnic or barbecue is always a good way to get folks acquainted. In between stops, by approval of the residents, entertainment activities such as playing games, dancing, or establishing an elevator band may be sanctioned.

Upon disembarking proper good-byes should be exchanged along with mailing addresses and promises to write soon. Each person exiting the elevator should be given a fond farewell, thanked for making the elevator ride an enjoyable experience, and wished well for the future. Hugs and handshakes while not mandatory are a nice touch. Similarly, parting gifts are not required.

Muzac. Is now considered tacky, if not illegal. If you wish music to accompany your ride on the elevator bring your own instruments and organize an elevator band. When forming a band keep in mind that people like music they can dance to.

In most cases, the chairman of the welcoming committee also serves as band conductor, however, a more musically experienced or inclined individual may be appointed as conductor by a simple majority vote of those on board.

Likewise, instruments should be tailored to the prevailing safety and space considerations. Concert grand pianos, pipe organs, and trombones are not recommended. Neither are accordions or banjos, not for any space or safety reasons, but because they are so annoying.

Emergencies. Many types of emergencies can occur while riding in elevators. The proper response to these emergencies depends on what type of emergency conditions are in effect. A simple mechanical malfunction causing a stop between floors may not require any committee action whatsoever. If the elevator stalls, don't panic, just have another elevator pull up alongside you. Then use jumper cables to give your elevator a jump start to get going again.

However, if the period of time is prolonged the committee can organize entertainment to pass the time. While the type of entertainment is up to the individual committees, good taste should be an overriding concern, and 'I Spy' is not a recommended past time.

If there is a threat of protracted internment, the committee can establish a resource rationing plan by acquiring any gum, candy, breath mints, water bottles, etc. from the occupants of the elevator to be apportioned on a fair and equitable basis. Under extreme conditions the committee chairperson can declare a state of martial law. At which point a hand selected sergeant-at-arms can be appointed by the chairperson and used to enforce order or ration resources.

Be warned, however, that the actions of such chairpersons under a state of martial law are subject to review by the entire committee when the occupants of the elevator are freed. The resulting investigation could result in the disbarment of that individual from ever holding an elevator chairmanship again.

Remember, regardless of the state of emergency, the guidelines listed in the United Nations Universal Declaration of Human Rights must be adhered to. A copy of this should be kept in the same compartment as the emergency phone (along with a copy of this guidebook).

Emergency phones. Emergency phones should at no time be used for personal calls, unless of course you can dial long distance. A seniority system based on the length of time spent in the elevator is used to determine who has first use of the phone.

Full Capacity. If the elevator is filled to capacity or deemed to be over capacity the committee may elect to expel the most junior members of the elevator committee in order to make the elevator ride safer and more pleasurable.

Unruly occupants. From time to time your elevator committee will have to deal with unruly and anti-social occupants. Unless your elevator is operating under martial law the following methods of dealing with them are recommended.

First, you should politely request that they cease and desist in their unruly activities.

Second, pull over and stop the elevator. Refuse to start it until they settle down. Finally, if all else fails, they can be expelled from the elevator by a two-thirds majority vote.

The following behavior is considered disorderly conduct.
1. Pretending no one else is in the elevator by staring at the floor display.
2. Refusing to take part in committee approved social functions.
3. Refusing to extend greetings of salutations to incoming or outgoing elevator occupants.
4. Not singing along or taking part in sanctioned functions.
5. Not trying the potato salad because they aren't sure how long it's been out.

The following is a list of offenses that may be grounds for expulsion.
1. Removing articles of clothing from yourself or other occupants of the elevator. (Unless it's mutually agreeable.)
2. Jumping up in the air as the elevator is proceeding down because it "feels neat."
3. Asking the other occupants, "Did your ears pop?" or "How fast can this thing go?"
4. Telling horror stories about elevator accidents.
5. Screaming, "We're all going to die!" when the elevator makes funny noises.

Elevator races. There exists a temptation for employees to organize and bet on elevator races. However, this is frowned upon, unless there is serious money riding on it.

When you should not ride an elevator. Elevators should be avoided in case of fire and rain. Riding elevators under the influence of alcohol or other drugs is strictly forbidden.

The emergency stop button. One may ask, why is there an emergency stop button in the elevator? It does not seem logical that a person would want to suddenly stop the elevator in between floors. The answer is rather simple, the emergency stop button is there in case anyone falls out of the elevator, you can stop the elevator and go back and pick them up.

If you are experiencing an emergency in the elevator and want it to end, simply press the emergency stop button and the emergency will stop.

Sex in the elevator. Sex in the elevator is expressly forbidden, as it may cause people to get off on the wrong floor.

CHAPTER 19
PARTIES AND
OTHER IMPORTANT OFFICE EVENTS

The office is more than a place to work, it's a place to party. As a corporate employee you will be expected to take part in the festivities and primitive rituals that surround the modern corporation.

Corporate parties are far less elaborate and extensive than they once were, but are still good for a few days in intensive care or detox.

While the modern office party may not be as grand or extravagant as some of its forerunners, they are often co-opted from traditions of unbridled reckless celebration held in pagan corporations with fertility festivals and the like. Actually, they haven't changed much at all.

The History of Corporate Parties

The first primitive corporations had virtually no parties at all as all activity was dedicated to survival. Over time, however, there developed within the corporate world certain ritualistic festivities.

By the beginning of the Neolithic Revolution, office parties centered around invoking the profit motive were quite common. The origin of the modern company party was a ritual designed to increase productivity and profits.

Holidays have always been a good time for an office party. Early corporations like the Pagan limited partnerships celebrated holidays on historically significant days steeped in tradition, like the winter solstice and vernal equinox.

By the time of the Roman Empire, corporate parties began to reach their zenith and no expense was spared in providing corporate employees with entertainment. It is widely held that the excesses of Roman office parties led to the ultimate collapse of the Roman corporate system, a.k.a. the Roman Empire, as more time and money was actually spent on parties than on corporate business.

The nature of the corporate holiday celebration has changed over time. The modern company is limited primarily to holidays where everyone can get a three day weekend. Many of these original meanings have been lost, as these corporate festivities have been passed from generation to generation.

The Modern Corporate Party

Now, we are left with a few of the more popular holiday parties including Christmas, New Year's Eve, and Release of Economic Indicators Day. This chapter is designed to aid you, in understanding what you as an employee should do in each of these office party situations.

The Christmas Party. This is the most well known and the most notorious of all the office parties. This should not give you the false assumption that it is indeed the most dangerous or troublesome type of office party to deal with. The reputation surrounding the Christmas Party is attributable to its popularly and longevity.

The Christmas Party actually predates Christmas. Pagan limited partnerships have celebrated the winter solstice since prehistoric times. So, no other party has been part of the corporate world for so long, nor has any other been so widely practiced. As a result, the stories revolving around the Christmas Party are bound to be the most embarrassing of all.

Like other corporate festivities the Christmas Party is based on celebrating the profit motive. The Christmas bonus is one method that has been traditionally used to get corporate employees in the Christmas Spirit.

This tradition of giving a bonus can be traced back to the Middle Ages when conquering CEO's rewarded their employees with the spoils of war like gifts of land, livestock, and women. Disloyal employees were often fired, literally. The purpose of doing this was to increase employee loyalty to the CEO and the corporation.

The modern Christmas Party is a similarly perilous affair. It is not uncommon for employees of all departments, with secretaries and executives alike, taking part. If you have a particularly large office one has to be cognizant of the fact that you do not want to accidentally or unintentionally insult one of your supervisors. Thus, you have to exercise a good deal of caution. Do not play any 'pranks' on someone until you have ascertained whether or not they can fire you.

Here are some ways to spot an executive at the office Christmas Party.
1. They don't pay for their refreshments,
2. They don't worry about who they are playing pranks on,
3. They act like they own the place (because they do), and
4. They wear nametags saying, Warning: Executive!

It is always wise to follow certain established rules of good conduct at office parties. While it is largely a case of anything goes, certain things are considered to be in poor taste and thus worth doing.

Some of these include,
1. Stuffing the microwave oven full of unpopped microwave popcorn, turning the microwave on high and screaming, "Avalanche! Run for your lives!"

2. Seeing how much eggnog it takes to fill up various sized articles of clothing, or

3. Wearing Christmas tree decorations and asking other employees if they'd like to "top the tree."

New Year's Eve. A close second to the Christmas Party, the New Year's Eve Party has established itself with quite a reputation. The primary reason for this holiday party is so that company employees can amass a large collection of scandalous and idiotic stories in a surprisingly short time span.

The New Year's Eve Party generally lasts much later into the night than the Christmas Party. Certainly, this is bound to be the case since the whole purpose of the celebration is to stay up past midnight to see if the New Year actually makes it. In reality like most holidays this is simply an excuse to drink and act like an idiot.

Unlike Christmas parties, New Year's Eve parties are more than annoying since you only have a day or two off at most to recover. Given the amount of fluids of various natures imbibed, this is a wholly inadequate amount of time to recover. A few simple thought out steps taken on the night of the party can easily extend the actual, if not official, vacation time.

The following are some possibly useful tactics.

1. Filling all the door locks with white out, epoxy, or similarly plugging substances,

2. Pouring eggnog into the phone system (preferably left over from the Christmas Party),

3. Pouring any sticky liquids on computer key boards creating all sorts of new electrical pathways with potentially humorous results,

4. Running appetizers through the automatic feed systems on office copy machines,

5. Using the office shredders to shred cheese and articles of clothing (not currently attached to any employee), or

6. Kidnapping an executive.

Birthdays. Birthday parties are the most interesting of all types of office parties. Rather than using a bank holiday as an excuse to do something in the office other than work, you are actually recognizing a fellow employee as another human being. This may be difficult, as sometimes it is hard to think of some employees as being human.

However, this can be used to your advantage. Given a fairly sizable office staff (and adding in a few extra days) you should be able to celebrate a birthday at least once every week. Celebrating these joyous events will greatly cut down the amount of time you have to work.

In giving presents to someone celebrating a birthday virtually anything goes. Some gift ideas that won't cost you anything include items you find in the lost and found or lying about the executive offices.

However, the following are presents that are considered in bad taste.
1. Office supplies,
2. Corporate promotional items, or
3. Things you found in the recipient's own office.

Showers. While these fall into several categories they share a great many similarities. Showers are primarily given in celebration of weddings and births (sometimes both and not necessarily in that order). These are generally not office parties that are officially sanctioned by the corporate higher ups, instead they really are an illegal use of office space. As a result, these tend to be clandestine operations involving a small number of collaborators. Even though they may be small, they can easily get out of hand.

The following are some ways to know when a shower has gone awry.
1. Shower gifts are items from your desk,
2. The shower party is going on its third day, or
3. Participants are actually in the shower. Together.

Release of economic indicators. In early agrarian corporations the changing of the seasons were the only economic indicators that really mattered. While this seems like a relatively new ritual, this holiday actually dates back to the tradition of the vernal and autumnal equinox, and the Summer and Winter Solstice celebrations which today have been very cleverly renamed the first, second, third, and fourth quarters.

In some ancient Roman corporations an animal would be sacrificed and their entrails would be analyzed by early economists. This provided them with divine revelation to foretell their future economic status, which is likely why they all went bust. Even so, this is not so different than what goes on in many corporations today.

As corporate life became more complex the seasons, the weather, and small animals were no longer the predominant economic indicators that governed corporate economic cycles. Nowadays, there are reams of incomprehensible data that governs corporate life. The release of these economic indicators, although not necessarily an official corporate event is nonetheless important news.

The mood of this event depends on the results of the economic indicators for a particular corporation. You may not understand what these indicators mean, but don't despair, neither do most executives. There are, however, a few subtle clues you can pick up based on the conduct of your company's executives.

The following are some of the signs that the recent economic forecast does not look good for your company.
1. Executives sit in their offices with the lights off quietly sobbing (not foolproof),
2. Executives haven't come into work for the last few days (not foolproof either), or
3. Executives come to work wearing black.

CHAPTER 20
IS THERE LIFE AFTER WORK?

Your working life does not only include your time on the job, but intrudes into your free time. Eventually, you will be forced against your will to do things with your coworkers outside of the office. After work activities cover a great deal of areas. Golf with the boss, drinks with your colleagues, and playing on the corporate softball team are all examples of after work activities that you will have to deal with.

Corporate Sports

In order to imbue the corporate spirit of teamwork into their employees many corporations have their own sports teams like softball, touch football, basketball, and the like. You will be asked, or maybe even gently required, unwittingly coerced, or tricked into taking part in some of these sporting activities.

Be careful, this is a very risky area. If you say no you run the risk of losing your job as playing sports are often more important to some executives than doing any actual work. If you say yes you run the risk of losing your life, or worse, vital body parts.

The history of corporate sports is as old as mankind itself. History has often mistaken these games for small wars. In fact, they were simply sporting events that got out of hand and resulted in some unfortunate casualties of corporate employees. While current intra-corporate sporting events seldom result in fatalities (except in some European countries), they still have the air of viciousness and savagery with which they began.

You may find the temptation to bean an executive in softball or 'accidentally' tackle them in touch football irresistible. A word of caution here, this may be your only chance to realize what many employees only dream about, hitting the boss.

Bear in mind that these types of sports may help the employees to get their aggressions and pent up feelings out. Thus, it is highly recommended that disliked employees and executives do not take part in these sporting activities. Studies indicate that there is a higher incidence of 'accidents' occurring to these people. If you fall into a category of disliked or despised colleague you may want to think twice before accepting an invitation to a game of rugby or mumblety-peg.

If, despite your best efforts, you get conscripted into a company sports team do not give up hope. There are several ways you can easily get out of being on any team.

Here are a few.
1. Play very, very badly,
2. Score points for the other team, and
3. 'Accidentally' injure your own teammates.

After a few non-serious, but nonetheless painful injuries you will undoubtedly be discharged from the team by everyone's mutual consent.

Sporting with the boss. The most commonly used method to get ahead is losing at golf to your boss. This is an absurd and overrated means of getting along with the person who has the power of life and death over you. You will not gain points by being seen as a loser in the eyes of your boss.

However, this does not mean you will succeed by beating your boss and rubbing his nose in it by saying things like, "You may be my boss, but I can beat the crap out of you at golf." He may not be able to beat you at golf, but he can fire you.

Instead, you should take a cue from the movies. Play well to begin with, get ahead, and then your boss can engineer a brilliant come from behind victory. It's not much fun to win all the time, or handily beat your underlings at sporting activities. (Actually it is.) Thus, it is important to give the impression of stiff, even superior competition your boss finally overcomes to win.

As a rule, you should avoid any sporting activities where there is the likelihood of fatal injuries. While the demise of your boss may be your ticket to getting ahead, police investigations are bound to see this as a motive that may result in some uncomfortable questioning.

It may be better to avoid going sporting with your boss all together. By avoiding a competition in the first place, you will likely be further ahead.

The following are some rough and ready excuses for not taking part in a sporting event with your boss.
1. Old football injury,
2. Old war injury, or
3. You've given it up for Lent. (In season only.)

Whatever you do decline all offers to go hunting with your boss. Especially if your boss does not like you. And no matter what he might say, it is not common practice to wear camouflage and antlers to stalk deer in the woods.

It is also a good idea to avoid boating, fishing, skiing, and doing anything that involves a propeller like on a plane or boat.

It is quite normal for people who work together to also play together. After hours of being together at the office, you will likely want to get together after work for even more hours of fun and excitement together.

This type of socializing may involve several types of functions.
1. Family gatherings,
2. Private parties, or
3. Cruising the town,

When your coworkers invite you to attend their family gatherings, avoid them like you would any contagious disease. These events often degenerate into something only slightly more fun than the Spanish Inquisition. At best they can be boring and irritating, at worst they are nearly fatal.

Private parties can range from dull to boring. Many times the purpose of inviting colleagues or fellow employees to these functions is to take the cost of the party as a business expense, rather than out of any desire to socialize with colleagues.

The practice of cruising the town is perhaps the oldest form of socialization outside of the office. Many are the cases of Viking corporate employees having one too many horns full of mead, getting blotted, and then sailing off to England to raid a monastery or some other such random escapade. On one such occasion, Viking employees got so drunk they sailed the wrong way and discovered the continent of North America, much to the surprise of the people already living there.

Convention
Agenda

1. Plunder
2. Pillage

CHAPTER 21
CONVENTIONS AND OTHER
ACTS OF CONTROLLED VIOLENCE

You will occasionally be required to take part in corporate activities beyond your place of work. As you move up the corporate ranks you'll be able to go on longer and better field trips away from the workplace, and some are even overnighters.

You will find this is one of the best excuses to get out of work and away from the spouse and kids by skipping out of the office under the guise of actually doing company business.

The History of The Convention

The convention has historically been one of the more popular means by which employees from many different corporations can get together to waste time and use up their expense accounts. Business trips, conventions, and the like grew out of the need to participate in these collective acts of controlled violence.

The convention business is quite lucrative so cities compete to attract corporate conventions. However, this was not always the case. Conventions used to be unpredictable, rowdy, and often violent. Actually, things haven't changed that much at all. What has changed is now cities actually want this to take place.

When the Normans decided to hold a convention in Britain in 1066, the Anglo-Saxon tourist board thought this was great. Unfortunately, the convention got out of hand and the Normans wound up conquering the country. Instead of just spending the weekend and going home, they stayed and their descendants live there to this day.

In a similar incident the Gaul's convention got out of hand in 390 B.C. and their high spirited antics culminated in the sacking and burning of Rome. History is filled with conventions gone wild, the sacking of Constantinople by the Crusaders in 1204 and the Democratic National Convention in Chicago in 1968, to name a few.

Like the convention, business trips have proven to be dangerous for all involved giving them a formidable reputation. After all, Genghis Khan was just taking a few corporate employees on a business trip and ended up conquering most of Asia.

The modern business convention is believed to have originated in the Middle Ages. After the fall of the multinational Roman Empire Corporations a power vacuum was created across Europe. This led to the flourishing of small startups and limited partnerships.

Over time, these new corporate startups would vie for more and more territory and customers. The corporate climate was dangerous as corporate raiders who were often mistaken for hordes of marauding barbarians roamed the countryside so executives had to become armored in order to protect themselves. This established the practice of executives wearing suits made out of armor.

As Europe emerged from the Dark Ages hostile takeovers began to be regulated to a greater extent. As these new corporations gained more market share they solidified their customer base and marketing territory making hostile confrontations less and less frequent.

Still, executives needed ways to increase their notoriety and prestige. So, in order to gain fame and glory they started to compete with other executives on a simulated field of battle. And so began the tradition of the modern convention.

In the first early conventions, sometimes called tournaments, two or more corporations would determine a time and place to meet. Since the convention center had not yet been invented, this often took place on a large field outside of town.

These events were surrounded by much pomp and pageantry. After much drinking and eating, and even more drinking almost to the point of the executives being incapable of seeing straight, the contests of skill would begin.

The executives of each corporation would line up facing one another, as if ready to do battle. They would then send their employees out into the battlefield to scrimmage with one another. These mock hostile takeovers would begin much as they still do today with both corporations sending their legal departments, sometimes called serfs, out to skirmish with one another.

After the legal departments beat each other senseless, the executives would yell "serf's up" (hence the origin of the term). Then other departments would rush each other and a great fracas would ensue on the field of battle.

Individual combat between corporate executives would follow the opening acts. Executives, or knights as they were called, were easily recognizable as they wore suits of armor, the forerunner of the modern business suit. The executives would engage in tests of individual skills with one another including hand-to-hand combat and jousting. Eventually, one side would beat the crap out of the other side.

Executives who were defeated would run away, bolting into the countryside. The victorious corporation would spend the rest of the day hunting them down and capturing them.

This ritual led to modern corporate recruiting practices and the use of headhunters. These early conventions proved to be so violent that they were banned by the church, which only made them even more popular.

The Modern Convention

The modern convention, like its predecessor, is a time of reverie, unfettered violence, and reckless abandon. The number of employees your company sends to a convention will depend on many factors. The least of which is how many employees it actually needs to send.

The general rule is that if the convention is in the Caribbean, Vegas, or any of a number of other tourist spots you are bound to have a strong contingent, especially of the executive grade. On the other hand, conventions in small agricultural towns will usually have small contingents.

If the convention is in a very popular tourist spot it is likely that there will be more employees wanting to go than is allowed by law. So there needs to be a fair and equitable means to decide who goes and who stays home.

The following are some criteria to determine who can attend the convention.
1. The employees who know the most about the subjects the convention covers,
2. By lottery (for a nominal fee per ticket), or
3. By who is related to the CEO.

Alternately, delegates to the less attractive convention locations are chosen by the following criteria.
1. Employees the CEO dislikes, but can't fire,
2. By drawing straws, or
3. The employees who were 'too good' to participate in the 'pranks' at the last convention.

Once you are at the convention the fun is just beginning. Chances are you are in a totally unfamiliar town. This can be an advantage for you. If the convention is boring and you are not familiar with a city it is quite easy to get lost.

For instance, if the convention is in Los Angeles you may accidentally wind up as a movie extra, a contestant on a game show, or on the beach. It may take several hours or even days for you to realize that you are not at the convention. With any luck by the time you realize this mistake it will be time to go home.

If for some reason you decide to show up at the convention, you will have to deal with people from many different companies. What makes this even more distressing is that this forces people together in a small confined space. Given the volatility of most corporate employees, the horror stories that accompany the attending of such conventions are to be expected.

To prevent things from getting out of hand, there are several types of strategies to keep the hordes of corporate employees from spilling out of the convention and plundering or pillaging any nearby cities. The following are just a few of these strategies.

The Oasis. The concept behind the oasis is to make the convention hotel more attractive than the nearby population centers, in the same way that an oasis is much more attractive than burning desert sands. This is a costly and rather difficult strategy to carry out, but some of the following enticements are generally used to keep people at the hotel.

Try the following.
1. Providing free cable television,
2. Providing free alcoholic beverages, or
3. Providing free promotional items like pens, mouse pads, or condoms.

The Labyrinth. Just as King Minos of Crete had a cunningly constructed maze built to trap the Minotaur, the purpose of the labyrinth strategy is to prevent the people attending the convention from getting out of the hotel by hiding the exits. The goal here is to confuse and disorientate anyone attending the convention.

Some of tactics employed to do this are as follows.
1. Mis-numbering the floor numbers in the elevators,
2. Putting EXIT signs on broom closets,
3. Locking the conventioneers into the convention hall, and
4. Putting PLEASE USE OTHER DOOR signs on all the exists from the building. (Bear in mind, however, that this tactic is generally frowned upon by the local fire marshal and may be in violation of lots and lots of local ordinances.)

The Local Emergency. This involves spreading the news that the nearby population center is in the grips of some deadly or dire emergency that would make the convention goers desire to stay away.

Some possibilities emergencies include,
1. Being closed for remodeling,
2. A natural disaster,
3. A national political party convention, or
4. A heavy metal concert.

Another possibility is the quarantine. This is a rather simple method of keeping the convention goers inside the hotel. Simply fabricate a health emergency and a reason to quarantine everyone in the building. Bear in mind, however, that this may greatly reduce the number of people coming to the hotel.

Your conduct at a convention is a reflection of your corporation, so act accordingly. If you are polite and well behaved it may reflect badly on your corporation's executives who may have a reputation to maintain. Don't let them down or you may end up leading a delegation to a 'new' convention in Siberia.

Certainly there is bound to be an exchange of corporate logos, pens, promotional items, clothes, bodily fluids, and the like at these conventions. However, any swapping or transferring of titles of rank (e.g. Executive Vice-President) is expressly forbidden and grounds for expulsion from the corporation.

In case of emergency the following excuses will not work as an explanation for the local police department.
1. I didn't know it was illegal,
2. I didn't mean to drop it off the balcony,
3. I was not trying to hit your squad car, and
4. Everyone else was doing it.

If the convention is in a foreign country, you should learn some phrases in the local language including,
1. Please and thank you,
2. I'm sorry,
3. I'd like those two big ones, and
4. What is the quickest way to the American embassy?

Prenup
tual
Agree-
ment

CHAPTER 22
SEX IN THE OFFICE

There is a part of corporate life that is older than the corporation itself. It permeates every part of our existence and is inescapable even in the cloistered world of the corporate offices. As you may have guessed from the chapter title this force is known as romance, okay sex.

The office romance has received mixed reviews over the centuries. It can take many forms including affection, infatuation, unrequited love, or unbridled lust. It can make your corporate life heavenly bliss or a living hell.

This chapter is designed to familiarize you with the various types of office romances you may encounter. It will give you some guidance on how to handle these new and strange feelings along with the unique problems associated with the office romance.

The office romance is a force to be reckoned with. It has been the subject of a great deal of research whose findings are reflected in phrases like "don't buy your candy where you buy your groceries" and "don't dip your pen in the company ink." Although no one is really sure what this means it may have something to do with a warning against sex in the office.

Romance is based on a concept not readily recognized in the corporate world, love. While executives do not deny the existence of love, they shrewdly point out that it doesn't show up on a balance sheet. This is largely due to the historical role that the office romance has played.

In Medieval times corporate executives used extra-office affairs to establish political alliances and trading connections with other corporations. They increased their power and wealth by marrying women with large assets.

Love and marriage was treated as a business deal in order to increase the power of an executive. It was also the means of producing an heir to become the next CEO after his father, the current CEO, was killed in battle. As a result, wives who could not produce heirs were all too often cast aside in favor of more profitable ones.

Because executives often had to marry for the good of the corporation, they were not able to develop romantic relationships base on true love. That is until the concept of the office affair was developed. Once executives learned they could 'have their Kate and Edith too,' so to speak, the office affair was off and running quickly becoming very popular.

Romance that is not for the benefit of the corporation, but for the personal feelings of just two individuals had its own complications. Now a wife would not just provide her husband assets, she could take them away as well. This led to the introduction of new contractual relations, like the prenuptial agreement. These developments recaptured a more corporate like approach to love and marriage that was pervasive in the early corporate world.

Many of our current romantic traditions date back to the Germanic corporations of the 3rd century. Male corporate employees would often marry women from their own company. However, if there was a short supply of eligible women a male employee and a trusted coworker would go raid another corporation seizing a suitable woman and her assets, then bring her back to their company.

Over time, this trusted coworker has been transformed into the best man of today. Similarly, the honeymoon period now largely ritualistic, was originally the amount of time the man had to hide his new acquisition while waiting for her coworkers to get tired of looking for her.

The Modern Office Romance

You may wonder how to recognize an office romance so you can determine if you are in the midst of one at the moment. In order to ascertain whether or not this is the case the following information will help to explain what an office romance involves. While people differ on its exact content most concur that an office romance consists of a series of progressive stages.

These stages are:
1. Determining your objective.
2. Making contact.
3. Negotiating an agreement.
4. Consummating the merger.
5. Closing the deal.

1. Determining your objective. If you are actively pursuing an office romance, determining your objective is one of the most important aspects of developing a relationship. You are bound to have a few characteristics that you particularly desire in mind.

These often include,
1. Compatibility,
2. A nice personality, or
3. Large assets.

Since you are looking for a lasting relationship with a beneficent and fruitful merger, it is important to get to know the person with whom you wish to have a romantic interest. Thus, you must act with care and discretion.

In order to make your office romance a more positive experience, you should look for a partner with these qualities.
1. Someone who can promote you,
2. Someone who can provide potential lucrative inside information, or
3. Someone who makes more money than you.

There will be times when you will have to deal with unwelcome advances. While this may be a difficult problem it is rather simple to fix. There are many ways of dealing with these advances.

These approaches are similar to what a corporation would do in the case of an unwelcome takeover attempt.
1. Play hooky,
2. Play dead, or
3. Run away.

You may want to avoid having a relationship with either a supervisor or a subordinate as this can make corporate life very difficult for both of you. This may put undue pressure on the relationship especially if one of you can fire the other for underperforming.

2. Making contact. You may well ask where is the best place in the office to find someone for a romance. While there is no rough and ready answer to this question the following places have been known to be successful.

1. The water cooler,
2. The employee lunchroom,
3. Personnel files (this will also let you find out how much they make for a living), or
4. The men's or women's restroom. (If you're a man wait outside the woman's restroom. You won't meet a woman in the men's restroom, unless of course, she's looking for romance too.)

3. Negotiating an agreement. After making contact the all too well known process of dating begins. At this point, you are trying to determine whether or not the person you have met has the qualifications you are looking for in the event of a possible merger.

While the time and place of the date is largely left to your discretion, the following are some rules that should be followed.
1. Do not date during office hours (your boss will not like it, unless you're dating your boss),
2. Do not take office work with you on the date, and
3. Do not take another backup date on the date.

While you are on a date you may wonder whether or not it is going well. Most of the time you should be able to determine whether or not the date is successful rather easily.

However, the following are indicants that your date is not going well.
1. The person you are on the date with is talking (to people at other tables),
2. The person you are on the date with is asleep (and you two are still at the restaurant),
3. The person you are on the date with went to the rest room (for 'just a minute' over two hours ago), or
4. The person you are on a date with just left with her "cousin" (who just happened to be there and couldn't remember her name).

A date can be considered successful, for the most part, if there is,
1. An exchange of personal information,
2. An exchange of expressions of affection,
3. An exchange of financial statements,
4. An exchange of medical records, or
5. An exchange of bodily fluids.

4. Consummating the merger. If dating has gone well the office romance enters into a stage of merger negotiations. During this stage both parties are attempting to establish the conditions of a possible merger. This is rather like the legal process of discovery where questions are exchanged and evidence is requested from the other party about their hopes, dreams, aspirations, and finances.

In this phase, the skills you honed as a corporate employee should come in handy. You, in essence, have to sell yourself. However, if you do not have a very marketable product do not be disheartened. The annals of corporate history are filled with hugely successful marketing campaigns for otherwise less then promising products. This has traditionally been done by offering coupons, discounts, rebates, and two-for offers.

5. Closing the deal. If negotiations go successfully it will be time to close the deal. What you do to close the deal varies from corporation to corporation so you should be sure to get everything in writing. You should consider your operating costs as some relationships are higher maintenance than others. It might be a good idea to get an extended warranty in case the relationship breaks down.

As a result, the growing use of prenuptial and other types of agreements have given closing the deal the formality of a corporate contractual arrangement. Using your corporate experience, there are several types of contractual agreements to consider like rent to own or pay as you go. You might include compensation for time and materials or admonishments for any failure to perform.

Chapter 23
Sleep Your Way to The Top

So, how do I become an executive? Many eager readers of this volume are saying to themselves, "it's about time!" After all, isn't getting ahead what every eager corporate employee wants to do? The answer clearly is yes, and no. The first subject to deal with is what does 'getting ahead' actually mean.

There are several measures of getting ahead. The two most important are,
1. Money (e.g. how large your salary is).
2. Status (e.g. how big your office is).

Actually, these are the only important measures of success. Getting ahead, however, is more than wanting a larger salary or higher position. But not much more. Getting ahead necessitates that you appear to be doing well, that people above you like you, and that you are able to beat out the competition.

Many young corporate employees enter their corporate life with dreams of rising to the top ranks of a corporation to become an executive. You too may have these yearnings for future fame and fortune in the upper echelons of the corporate hierarchy.

You may ask, "How do I get on top? Sleeping your way to the top is a time honored tradition. So, take two or three warm blankets, a comfortable pillow, sleeping bag, and air mattress to work. Corporations like employees who sleep around the office because a comatose employee generally makes fewer mistakes than an alert one.

So, are you executive material? This is the most obvious question to be asked. Naturally, you will probably say yes without a moment's hesitation. But have you really thought about whether or not you could function properly and efficiently as a corporate executive?

Are You Executive Material?

So, if you really want to aspire to be a corporate executive in today's corporate world take the following self-test to determine whether or not you are executive material.

Rate yourself from 1 to 5 for each item. Five is excellent which is the highest rating and 1 is the lowest for poor. Similarly, 4 is very good, 3 is good, and 2 is fair.

When you are done add up your score. The higher your total score the more likely you may be executive material.

The following questions will help determine your general qualifications.
1. Do you have a briefcase and more than one suit?
2. Can you stay awake through long and boring meetings?
3. Can you look calm and collected when everything's in chaos?
4. Are you good at losing at golf?
5. Are you good at ignoring employees, even the attractive and seductive ones?

The following questions will help determine your communication skills.
1. Are you good at testifying?
2. Can you lie with a straight face?
3. Are you not easily intimidated by investigative journalists?
4. Can you give official statements to the media without perspiring profusely?
5. Are you able to speak in complete sentences without people understanding what you are talking about?

The following questions will help you to determine your business skills.
1. Are your interests superficial and don't last very long?
2. Can you keep your office neat and clean by not letting time consuming work get in your way?
3. Can you appear to be working on something at all times?
4. Do you appreciate the beauty of art, music, and stock options?
5. Can you be faithful to your corporation and the profit motive forsaking all others?

The following questions will help you to determine your leadership skills.
1. Do you have the ability to jump from task to task without actually finishing anything?
2. Do you face difficult decisions by pretending you're ill?
3. When you make a mistake can you be professional and blame someone else?
4. Do you enjoy the company of accountants and lawyers, even obnoxious and irritating ones?
5. Can you supervise employees without showing your animosity toward them?

The following questions will help you to determine your personal skills.
1. Do you feel others are out to get you?
2. Can you avoid dressing better than your boss?
3. Are you able to change deep rooted convictions on a moment's notice?
4. Can you keep the facts from unduly influencing your decisions?
5. Are you able to not let your sense of fair play interfere with your actions?

Once you have finished it should be self-evident how you did. However, bear in mind that if you have cheated and not answered these questions in a fair and honest manner you're just the sort of executive material some corporations are looking for.

Get Your Idea Approved

As hard as it may be to believe based on the behavior of some executives, if you want to become an executive eventually you will have to present your ideas to others.

You may think that your idea will stand on its own merits, but think again. The corporate world is a strange and forbidding place. Just because your idea would result in more efficient operations, lower costs, or increased profits does not mean it will be adopted or even considered.

Conversely, some of the stupidest ideas are taken to heart in the corporate world with disastrous consequences. You might well ask, what gets one idea adopted and another rejected if it's not the merit of the idea? The answer is simple. It's all in how you present your idea to your boss. This section should help you get your idea implemented and your achievements recognized despite the best efforts of your colleagues to stop you.

Eventually your boss is going to ask for your assistance in a decision or policy making capacity. More often than not he will ask you to analyze different approaches to a problem he can't solve for himself. To get him to pick the one that is the most beneficial to you, only give him a limited number of solutions to choose from. Encourage him to select the solution you want him to choose by presenting the other choices as unworkable or as repugnant as possible.

The key to making this to work is by only giving your boss the information he really needs to know. In other words, the information you want him to know. In essence this gives your boss only one real choice. After all, if he has all the facts he might start thinking for himself. If executives know too much they could be captured by rival corporations and tortured (or offered higher salaries).

While relatively uncommon, spontaneous glimmers of independent thought have been known to occur in the corporate world. A word of warning, in some instances developing ideas on your own is grounds for dismissal.

However, most bosses try to ignore such inspiration. If you find that you have had an independent thought and come up with a better way to do something you have set yourself on a difficult road. Corporations, especially large ones, are not known for their innovative techniques.

If you want to get ahead you have to learn the right lingo. There is some corporate jargon that will help you get what you want. Conversely, there is some jargon that if you use it, it will get ideas rejected.

You can use this jargon to your advantage to stop ideas you don't want to be approved. By using this jargon you can get your ideas approved to get ahead and the ideas your rivals come up with rejected.

Corporate jargon to use if you want your idea approved.
1. On time.
2. Under budget.
3. Environmentally friendly
4. Sex (While this most likely has nothing to do with your idea, studies show it can persuade people to do just about anything)

If there is an idea you want rejected, add this corporate jargon to it.
1. Over deadline.
2. Over budget.
3. Environmentally harmful.
4. Liability. (While this most likely has nothing to do with this idea, studies show this word scares people away.)

While at first glance these two lists seem to be the opposite of one another, in corporate jargon they are actually much the same. For example, ideas are always (not always) presented as coming in on time and under budget, but they rarely do and everybody knows it. They are more likely to end up over budget and run past their deadline, but being honest by saying so is likely to get your idea rejected and you possibly fired.

In presenting your idea to your boss there will be one of two results.
1. He will hate your idea.
2. He will love his new idea.

If the later occurs you have the choice of letting your boss proceed with his new idea or trying to convince people that it's your idea, while looking for a new job.

Other people besides you will be asked to present their ideas to the boss and you may be asked for your opinion about them. You should be prepared to find fault with them without resorting to phrases like, "it sucks" which tends to be ineffective and will only get you in trouble. There are many ways to sabotage your competition if you are going to get ahead in the corporate world.

Here are some standard ways to undermine the ideas of your opponents.
1. The legal department is raising questions,
2. It is economically or environmentally unsound,
3. The government is implementing a similar program, or
4. It's printed on the wrong type of paper.

If you fail to discredit the idea itself, turn your attention to the person who thought of it. Tell his boss that,
1. He wants to get you (his boss) fired so he can get your (his boss's) job,
2. He wants a better position in a rival corporation,
3. He is really an environmentalist, or
4. He plans to run for public office.

If all else fails forget about trying to argue rationally, go for broke. While these are not recommended, you might accuse your opponent of being any of the following. (In order of severity).

1. Communist,
2. Idolater,
3. Adulterer, or
4. Former government employee.

Going Over Your Boss's Head

For various and sundry reason, (i.e. to get promoted and make more money) you may have to go over your boss's head. Whether it's to score points, put yourself in line for promotion, or trying to get your boss fired proceed with care.

It is important to be very careful in going over your boss's head so that you are not seen as intentionally trying to upstage your boss. In some cases, this may be extremely difficult especially if you have a particularly lethargic boss. There are several ways you can go about going over your boss's head.

The most commonly used ways are as follows.

1. The direct approach,
2. The concerned approach, or
3. The anonymous approach.

The direct approach can be characterized by Farragut's immortal words, "Damn the torpedoes, full speed ahead!" This approach pays no heed to caution or to personal feelings and any possible consequences. This "do or die" attitude offers no compromises and expects none in return, this is a battle to the bitter end.

It is also the simplest way to go over your boss's head since you just go directly to his supervisor. If you chose this approach you had better make sure that you have enough dirt, we mean, information to do the job properly. A wounded and cornered boss is dangerous and deadly.

The following are a few ways to discredit your boss with his supervisor. Tell your boss's supervisor that,

1. He was planning to go over his head,
2. He has hired a 'contractor' from Vegas to 'take care' of him,
3. He dresses up at night in a cape and tights to 'fight crime,' or
4. He is planning to overthrow the corporation and establish a socialist state.

The concerned approach. This method is usually the most effective since it offers plausible deniability. It is also the more corporate like approach since it is far more insidious and sneaky than the direct approach. Using this approach, you go see your boss's supervisor for a 'quiet word' about something that concerns you greatly.

Some of possible concerns are,
1. He doesn't work and play well with others,
2. He's mentally unstable,
3. He's lost all interest in the profit motive, or
4. He's a former member of Congress.

The anonymous approach. This method involves many of the things already talked about. Anonymous letters or memos sent to your boss's supervisor along with relevant documents or photographs are very common methods of anonymously going over your boss's head. In order for the anonymous approach to work you must make sure that no one knows who sent the information.

As a result we recommend you avoid the following.
1. Using personalized stationary,
2. Mailing the anonymous letter from the same city you live in,
3. Signing your name, or
4. Bragging to your coworkers how clever you are. (If they know, they may tell your boss to try to get rid of you.)

So, despite your best efforts to get rid of your boss the result is that your boss gets a bonus or a promotion. If this happens you can sharpen your leadership skills by going underground and organizing your fellow coworkers to overthrow your boss. You will feel the thrill of being part of an underground resistance of freedom fighters within the company hierarchy fighting behind the lines for the integrity of your way of life.

Your departmental call will be your battle cry and your corporate logo will be your battle standard. A well executed reign of terror involving disabling coffee machines, putting chewing gum under desks, flushing important documents down the toilet, and jamming copy machines should bring company higher-ups to their knees forcing them to recall your boss and retreat.

Chapter 24
Good Executives Do It

Congratulations on becoming an executive! (Assuming you did become an executive.) Becoming an executive is the pinnacle achievement of the corporate world. Now that you are an executive you may have to take over the reins of power. However, you may be getting in over your head and not understand what's going on. If this is the case, don't be discouraged, companies frequently promote this type of person.

When you become the boss chances are that you will hear rumors of infidelity, embezzlement, alcoholism, sexual misconduct, and other vicious gossip. Don't be alarmed, this often happens because the other executives are jealous of your new promotion. So, just let them brag.

Corporate executives are the officer corps, the upper classmen of the corporate world. In this capacity you will now have certain powers and privileges of your station that are not available to low level employees. These perks are given in recognition of a person's accomplishments and dedication to the corporation, or simply because they are related to the CEO.

These are some of the powers and privileges granted to executives.
1. Their own parking space close to the building,
2. Keys to the executive washroom,
3. The ability to declare martial law in their department,
4. The power to impound employee's lunches when they are hungry, and
5. The right to flog underlings.

Taking Over a Department

In earlier times, upon taking over a department or corporation an executive would have their rivals and their rival's underlings put to death by some ritualistic means such as garroting, beheading, or disembowelment.

This practice is frowned upon nowadays, but for your own safety you should fire all employees who were loyal to the former boss. You have to act quickly to concentrate power before they know what's going on and try to overthrow you.

As a corporate executive you may have to take over the operations of an existing department. This can be very tricky so, you will have to learn everything you can about the department. You will certainly want to find out what kind of department you are getting yourself into, but more importantly you need to know how big your budget is and where the slush funds and petty cash are kept.

You will want to find out under what circumstances the former department executive left. Some possibilities include,

1. Fired,
2. Promoted,
3. Quit,
4. Run out of the office by their employees, or
5. Missing in action.

If the former department head was forcibly removed by his employees or is listed as missing in action, you may want to think twice about accepting the new position.

As a corporate executive you will not only have to continue to deal with the people above you, but now you will have to deal with the people below you as well. You will have to make choices about who to employ. You will have to decide how to use assistants to help you accomplish tasks given to you by the CEO.

There comes a time when every executive hires an assistant. The watchword for this process is caution. Remember, Brutus was Julius Caesar's assistant. The rule nowadays is not to have one primary assistant who becomes a threat to your position, but two assistants who spend their time fighting and bickering with each other preventing them from becoming a threat to you.

When you take over a department you may find several people on the payroll that no one in the office has ever seen. Be careful not to report them as they may be related to the CEO or they might be some executive's mistress or bookie. None of which you want showing up on the doorstep of your home in the middle of the night for a "chat."

As an executive, you might find out the work your employees are supposed to do exists only on paper. Their offices may not actually exist. You may come to realize that the whole department you are taking over exists only on paper as a tax write off. Don't panic, you have the ideal job. Fewer employees means fewer mistakes and less actual work for you.

Leadership Styles

As an executive, you will need to adopt a leadership style. Each one has its own strengths and weaknesses.

History offers us three major styles of leadership.
1. Egalitarian,
2. Liberal, and
3. Dictatorial.

Egalitarian. The cultural foundation of the western world stresses this brand of leadership style. It is based on the belief that everyone should be equal. Decisions tend to be discussed and policies considered by so many people that progress is greatly slowed down. The aim of this style of leadership is to allow for individual thought and democratic decisions, which is why it leads to so many problems.

However, once you have gained power you don't so much lead as draw a paycheck because as an Egalitarian leader, you can't actually change anything, even if you ran on a platform of 'change.' So, you end up leaving your employees up to their own designs and hope that something might get done, eventually, someday.

Like politicians you too can fill up you time fund raising and going on junkets to other corporations locally and abroad. A junket is a type of all-expense paid field trip, usually at someone else's expense (not yours), often at the public's expense. The main benefit of the Egalitarian leadership style is that it frees up your time to practice your golf game or go on executive junkets to ostensibly visit other corporations.

Benefits of the Egalitarian leadership style.
1. Always having time for golf,
2. Always having time for fund raisers, and
3. Always having time for overseas junkets.

Risks of the Egalitarian leadership style.
1. Not always being well liked,
2. Not always getting returned to office, or
3. Being criticized in the press.

Liberal. While this might look like an open-minded, tolerant, enlightened approach, it is actually a dictatorial leadership style in disguise because as a liberal you know what is best for everyone else and they better do what you say, or else. When you are a liberal you can be assured that you are always right, even when you are wrong. People will support you no matter what distasteful things you may say or do.

Being a Liberal style leader will automatically make you,
1. Smarter,
2. More sophisticated, and
3. Better looking. (Whether you are or not.)

Risks of the Liberal leadership style.
1. Being well liked,
2. Always getting returned to office, or
3. Getting your own television show.

Dictatorial. This leadership style is the historical model of the corporate executive. Decisions made by the CEO are passed down to his executives and then on down to his employees where they are ruthlessly enforced. This leader does not tolerate any deviation from the plan he lays out.

All dissenters, non-conformists, and opponents are dealt with harshly and strictly. As long as the reign of terror is maintained everything proceeds as intended. However, there is a tenancy for mutinies and executions of corporate officers to occur.

Benefits of the Dictatorial leadership style.
1. Actually getting people to do something,
2. Actually getting something accomplished, and
3. Actually being right.

Risks of the Dictatorial leadership style.
1. Being right (people don't like that),
2. Being overthrown by a populist revolt, (orchestrated by an Egalitarian style leader), or
3. Having your company "overthrown" by a "Democratic" style leader.

Subordinates, Lackeys, and Underlings

When you first meet your new underlings, (you probably don't want to call them underlings to their faces, at least not so soon) you will want to have someone they know introduce you to them because employees can be skittish about new department heads. You should be sure to tell them how enthusiastic you are about them and be careful about making any changes too soon.

There are times when your employees may not be doing what they are supposed to do. In some cases employees may have problems in their corporate life that you will have to deal with. They may come from single boss departments or from limited partnerships that have split up and the partners have gone their separate ways.

As a result, some employees may feel a great deal of distrust and may be reluctant to form emotional attachments to a new executive. Sadly, employees who have not had proper executive guidance may not know how to deal fairly with other employees so they will not have developed traditional corporate values. You will have to be sympathetic to these employees since they are a product of a broken department.

How to recognize signs of a troubled employee.
1. Do they amble around the office aimlessly, not working on anything in particular? (More so than normal.)
2. Do they refuse raises or promotions?
3. Do they act in a fair and equitable manner?
4. Do they ignore the profit motive?
5. Do they seem to have lost interest in things that once preoccupied them like coffee breaks, sports, gambling, or drinking?
6. Is there an increased incidence of 'accidents' in the office?

There are bound to be those employees who are intimidated with the corporate world and respond in strange ways to this threatening environment.

The following are just a few of the most common types of troubled employees you might have to deal with.

Blamers. This employee will maturely attribute all of their failures to circumstances beyond their control. The account was lost not due to their goofing off at work, but because the client was a "childish doody-head." Similarly, they didn't get the promotion because the boss has his favorites in the office. While this is true, it's essential that as few people as possible actually know it.

Bully. Sometimes, you will be confronted with the office bully. This type of employee goes around extorting lunch money from his colleagues by threatening to file their head under the letter H. (For head.) Most bullies are all talk, but if the bully in question is actually capable of carrying out this threat, you may want to make him your assistant.

Clown. Occasionally you will have to deal with the office clown. This is the sort of employee who will actually try to file his head under H in the filing cabinet. Once they gain attention through this kind of behavior this becomes their standard mode of conduct. Unchecked, escalation of this behavior can lead to chaos and damage to office equipment that could end up getting them promoted.

Dreamers. This person is usually totally absorbed in dreaming about what they are going to do. As a result, they spend countless hours with their feet up on their desk smugly smiling to themselves, going over in their mind how they will run everything. Don't listen to them, unless they really are in charge.

Self-indulgent. This employee tends to feel that they have to do more work than everyone else. This can make them act depressed and resentful. In reality, they often spend their time pursuing their own pleasure showing little self control or restraint. This is why you will usually find them in the legal department.

Radical. This employee may take up ideological causes like helping the environment or the community. This kind of activity needs to be stopped before it catches on. This behavior is not acceptable because the rebel is merely indulging in it to gain status or prestige in the corporation. That's what you need to do.

Yes Men. Actually yes men aren't so much troublemakers as employees who agree with their boss in order to curry favor with him. This can make them generally despised by their colleagues because they tend to be more frequently promoted. Be sure to protect yourself when having discourse with them as they may be saying yes to every executive they meet.

As an executive you will be called upon to deal with a wide variety of infractions by your employees. The following are a few of the most common employee troubles.

Cheating. Cheating among employees is to be expected because it is one way to get ahead in the corporate world. If you find an employee who is cheating and getting away with it, you should bring this to the immediate attention of your CEO as he will probably want to promote him.

Inattentiveness. You want to make sure that you have your employees' full attention, which may take some time. Unfortunately, most employees have a very short attention span. So, you may want to keep work activities to ten minutes or less.

Lying. To some in the corporate world lying can come as easily as breathing. You may overhear an employee boasting that his uncle is a "big executive in this corporation." He may simply be looking for more attention, however, before taking any disciplinary action you may want to make sure that he doesn't actually have an uncle who is a big executive in the corporation.

Stealing. Reported thefts can exceed the actual number of thefts because employees often accidentally, on purpose, lose or throw out their stapler, computer, or desk chair so that they will have to get a new one.

Uncorporate-like conduct. The corporate way of life must be preserved so any uncorporate-like behavior is the thin end of the wedge. Unchecked, it can lead to the collapse of the corporate world as we know it and encourage the growth of government.

Bad language. There will come a time when you have to deal with your employees' use of bad language. Do not simply ignore this because you may learn some new words. Employees have a tendency to say naughty words and once they get going, they may be difficult to stop and before you know it they get promoted above you.

There can be many reasons why employees say naughty words.
1. Because they want to fit in,
2. Because they want attention,
3. Because they might not know what it really means, or
4. Because they heard the older employees say it.

Whatever you do, don't overreact. This might be just the sort of employee the public relations department is looking for.

The New Employee

Sooner or later you will need to recruit new employees for your department. If your corporation does not recruit new employees it will eventually die out. Different corporations have taken different approaches to solve this problem. The traditional method of recruiting was through capturing them in war or through procreation. Given today's employment laws, these methods are no longer used to produce new employees.

Around the second millennium B.C. the Assyrians, Hittites, and Medes brought a new recruiting method into practice. In order to build larger and stronger corporations they would raid other corporations and carry their employees off to distant branch offices to work for them.

Similarly, they would bring employees from their home office to take over the corporate offices of the people they conquered. This practice still continues today, but under the name of executive placement. Instead of abducting the entire office staff, only the most pliable or most attractive employees are enticed away with offers of higher salaries and greater power.

When someone new joins your department they will have to go through your department's rites of passage such as initiation ceremonies that can turn ordinary civilians into something unrecognizable. Initiation ceremonies should be as imposing and forbidding as possible. If the class of new employees is large, the initiation ceremony can take place on a stage or in the cafeteria so their parents and family members can attend.

The room should be very dark, lit only by candles or other weak source of light. The new employee is brought in by a corporate executive. For maximum effect, bring them from a well lighted area so they are plunged into darkness as they enter the room. It will take several minutes for their eyes to adjust to the darkness. They will then see the dimly lit faces of their future coworkers.

Each department will have its own specific oath to be taken during the ceremony. The content of these oaths, while divergent, should include swearing allegiance to the corporation, penalties if they abandon their corporation, and usually some passages in arcane languages such as Latin and Sanskrit. Alternately, if no one in your corporation has knowledge of any ancient languages get the legal department to type something up. With any luck it should be totally incomprehensible.

Stages of Employees

One of the most emotionally fulfilling things you will do as the head of a department is bringing a brand new employee into the office. However, you must be aware how your older employees will react to the new arrival. They may see the new little guy as a rival for your attention and affection.

They may be jealous that you are spending more time training him than you are spending with them. To spare their feelings, it might be best to send your older employees out on errands or a long coffee break the day your new employee arrives.

After the new employee gets settled your old employees can be let back into the office. As the boss, you should do your best to give some of your undivided attention to each one of your older employees. Explain to them that the arrival of the new employee doesn't mean you love them any less.

Try not to fuss over the new employee too much when your older employees are around as it may hurt their feelings. Your older employees may become jealous when they see you training the new employee and may pester you to go through new employee training again with them. You should do what they want so they get it out of their system and they will quit when they become bored because employee training isn't as fun as they thought.

If company executives keep coming into your department and asking, "How's the new employee doing today?" or "Where's that darling new employee?" ask them to stop it because it can lead to feelings of resentment. Your older employees may no longer want to go visit their corporate executives if they see them fussing over the new employee.

During the first few months a new employee needs a lot of attention from his boss. This is the best time to bond with your new employee. A smile or a few words of encouragement is what they live for so this is a good time to get them to do what you want them to do.

However, a new employee can easily become overactive, even disruptive especially during meetings as their attention span is short and their interests quickly change. They may lose interest in what they are doing and demand more interesting work. They can seem to have limitless energy, running all over the office getting into everything. However, too much work can make them overly tired and cranky so they will need to take frequent naps.

As the new employee gets more accustom to his new surroundings, his imagination can run wild. He may rearrange the office furniture and call it his fort. So it can be helpful to give him his own space, perhaps his own desk or locker.

You may see him at his desk one minute, the next he is stalking a fellow employee pretending to be a big game hunter. He may run off and hide, then jump out and surprise you. During this time it can be helpful to try out different office activities to see which ones he likes best. Keep activities to a set limit as he can easily get overexcited and may have difficulty sleeping.

As a boss, you will eventually find yourself having to have 'the talk' with your new employee. There will come a time when one of your employees will ask, "Where do employees come from?" This can be an awkward situation. It can embarrass even the most experienced executive.

How you answer depends on the employee's level of maturity. You don't need to go into great detail. You might try saying something like, when an executive really cares about a company they can have a new employee.

This sidestepping the question will only work for so long and your employee may grow impatient, especially if they have heard the older employees talking about where new employees come from.

The older employees may make up stories to embarrass the new employee by telling him things like new employees are found in the parking lot or they come by air mail. This can frighten and confuse the new employee. If they persist on asking you where new employees come from, tell them to go ask the human resources department, because that's what they are there for.

After being employed for some time you will begin to notice changes taking place in a new employee. He is likely to distance himself from his boss and seek more approval from his coworkers, or whoever can provide him the most benefits. He will become increasingly interested in doing things with his peers like coffee breaks, elevator races, and betting pools.

He is likely to become sarcastic and disrespect authority figures like the CEO just to impress his coworkers. He may even identify with a particular department or gang who all dress alike in radical clothing, like wearing blazers or bowties.

You must keep a watchful eye on a new employee at this stage of his development since while on one hand he might act like a full fledged corporate employee, he can quickly relapse into less mature ways of doing things.

He will try to assert his independence so you may have to allow him a greater range in choosing and planning his own projects or he may come to resent you. He will insist that you drop him off down the block so his coworkers don't see him with you, but that doesn't mean he won't still ask to borrow the car.

At this stage, you can try to sway his loyalty by offering him more responsibility. In this manner, you can transfer this clique solidarity to the corporation and thus to you. Encourage your employee to identify with the corporation and to understand his duty to it. This is a good time to introduce him to the thrills of increased corporate profits, corporate raiding, and management training.

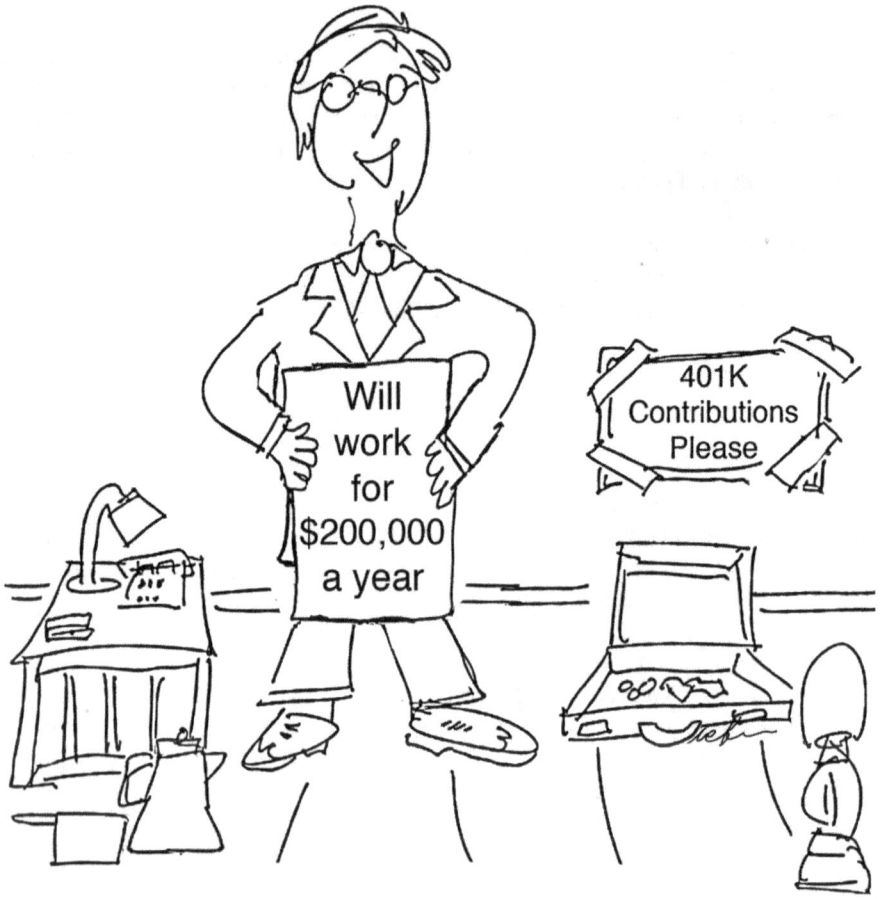

CHAPTER 25
YOU SCREWED UP!

Sooner or later, it happens to everyone. Confronted with the harsh reality of making a mistake you wonder, quite naturally, what you should do. Learning to deal with your mistakes is perhaps one of the most important of all corporate skills. It is the one that separates those who get ahead from those who get left behind.

Your choice of how to deal with your mistake depends on what type of mistake you have made. The following sections cover some of the more common errors that you are likely to make.

Simple accounting errors are perhaps the least hazardous of all screw ups. They can be blamed upon things that most executives don't understand and even fear, like computers or other 'technical stuff.'

Be warned, however, that these simple accounting errors are less generously accepted by real auditors or accounting firms. If you are worried about getting caught in double entry bookkeeping, we suggest an extended vacation to South America.

Certain traditions govern the life of an executive so if you transgress them, look out. Letting little things slip out during board meetings like, "why do we always have to find a way to shelter our income?" can result in alienation from your colleagues.

The following are some customs that must not be transgressed.
1. Questioning why the corporation has to get bigger profits every year,
2. Questioning why the corporation should oppose governmental regulation,
3. Refusing raises or promotions,
4. Not providing credible alibis for other executives, or
5. Humming jingles of rival corporations during meetings. (Not because executives dislike other corporation's jingles, but because humming is so annoying.)

Personally affronting your CEO or other executives can lead to sudden dismissal. The following are some of the more dangerous personal affronts.
1. Insulting your CEO,
2. Insulting your CEO's spouse,
3. Dumping drinks on your CEO at the office party,
4. Dumping your CEO on the drinks at the office party, or
5. Describing your CEO's ancestry in terms of primates.

Dealing with Your Mistakes

Whatever mistake you make, you can make it fit one of these options to deal with it.
1. Ignore it.
2. Cover it up.
3. Panic.
4. Quit.

1. Ignore it. The most natural inclination seems to be to ignore your mistake and hope that it goes away. This method may or may not work depending on what kind of mistake you have made. If the mistake is relatively small, it may be easy to ignore and sweep under the rug. Minor mistakes like overbilling clients may not be noticed for weeks or even years.

If the mistake is a simple numerical mistake chances are most bosses and executives have an innate distrust of computers to begin with and think of them as unreliable. Unfortunately, this has been a much overused excuse and so has lost much of its effectiveness.

If the offense is more serious, like misspelling your boss's name, it may be more difficult to avoid executive wrath. Similarly, if you are implicated in leaking information to the media that is inherently damaging to the corporation, it may not be enough to try to ignore the problem. Whatever the mistake, as soon as it is noticed this defense loses its effectiveness.

2. Cover it up. Many executives, especially the old school of type, consider the mistakes of subordinates to be the responsibility of their boss. (Unless of course it's their subordinate's mistake.) As a result, they may choose to make an example of whoever made the mistake to keep the other employees on their toes.

You can cover your tracks by going on the offensive and circulating a memo stating the mistake has come to your attention and you are looking for the person responsible for it. (Knowing full well it is you.)

If you have to, you can announce your findings. These are a few options.
1. Blame it on the computer,
2. Blame it on a coworker,
3. Blame it on the temporary help,
4. Blame it on corporate spies, Bolsheviks, wood sprites, gremlins, or saboteurs.

Blaming your mistakes on the computer is a good excuse because no one really understands how they work. However, doing this has become overused and cliché. Also a computer department employee may be offended and beat the crap out of you with a hard drive, because that's what they are really for.

Blaming your colleagues takes the heat off of you, temporarily, but results in increased departmental hostility and the issue may not necessarily end there. Chances are that your colleague won't idly accept the blame, but will try to shift the blame to someone else (possibly even to you), which may result in the higher-ups trying to determine who actually did make the mistake.

Blaming the mistake on persons unknown is fairly effective. It does not engender the same negative reaction in your coworkers since you are not putting the blame on anyone in particular. Temporary employees often get the blame because once the mistake is discovered they are often on to their next job so they can't be fired.

Corporate spies, Bolsheviks, wood sprites, gremlins, or saboteurs are useful non-entities who can be easily blamed for just about anything. Chances are your corporate executives will be flattered to think that someone thinks that they are important enough to be infiltrated by spies or saboteurs. This excuse provides a great deal of ego boosting for the CEO.

3. Panic. If all these choices fail to avert attention away from you, it's time to panic. People will say, "don't panic," but they couldn't be more wrong. Panicking provides you with adrenalin so you can do what needs to be done, to do things you other wise wouldn't do, and to take on your enemies.

It's time to take the offensive and bring the mistake to an executive's attention. Tell him that you have every intention of getting to the bottom of it, (before some nosey busybody finds out you are to blame).

By attacking the problem head on you should avert suspicion from yourself. Hopefully, not wanting to have any major problems, an executive who is also trying to hide his own mistakes will sweep your mistake under the rug for you.

Using this method you can beat your boss to the punch by setting up your own review and investigation committee. This committee need not necessarily consist of anyone other than yourself. Limiting membership as much as possible increases the chances of the committee coming up with the decision you want them to.

Hopefully, it won't be necessary for you to ever issue a report attributing any blame for the mistake. Most executives will be satisfied with a simple, "the matter is being looked into."

You might also try some tried and true responses politicians use when they panic.
1. Blame it on a right wing conspiracy,
2. Blame it on the liberal media,
3. Move to Australia, or
4. Emphatically insist that you did not have sexual relations with that woman.

4. Quit. If all efforts to hide your mistake or blame others fail, you might have the impulse to threaten to resign knowing that all will be forgiven because they really like you and want you to stay. Wake up! Doing this is not recommended since more often than not your CEO will take the easy way out and accept your resignation. Quitting cuts right to the heart of the matter and saves your CEO the time and trouble of building a case for dismissal.

The final and harshest choice you have is to admit your mistake. However, it is not necessary to come right out and admit that you made a mistake.

Here are several methods that can help you.
1. Calmly explain the mistake,
2. Blame it on stress and troubles at home,
3. Plead temporary insanity, or
4. Beg for mercy.

Calmly explaining the mistake is a toss of the dice. It may be accepted or rejected. You may be castigated and fired, or promoted for your forthright attitude.

In today's psychologically sensitive corporate world the once unacceptable excuses of stress and home life are now quite openly embraced. Be forewarned, however, that many corporations in a desire to be trendy have instituted a number of programs to encourage you to take part in a hideous form of mind control like rehab or counseling. While this may get you off the hook over your mistake, it may prove to be more than you bargained for in ruining your corporate life.

If you plead temporary insanity, you may find yourself temporarily unemployed. Alternately, and far more hideously you may be asked to take part in group therapy. This shocking method of group control was first used in a corporate capacity by the Mongol CEO Genghis Khan and has since been banned by most international treaties.

By using group therapy, Genghis transformed a relatively docile, local nomadic limited partnership, primarily interested in yogurt production, into one of the fiercest assemblages of multinational corporate raiders that the corporate world has ever known.

Begging for mercy has one major factor going for it, it appeals to your CEO's sense of omnipotence. However, it does not always translate into success. Your CEO may think you are merely a groveling, cringing, spineless excuse for a human being. But then again, that might be just the kind of executive he wants.

Chapter 26
Farewell
Get Even, Then Get Out

Sadly, all good things must come to an end. Actually, bad things must come to an end too, we just don't feel so bad about it. Despite your best efforts to placate everyone you may end up on your CEO's hit list. Rather than directly axing you, he may be taking a more insidious approach by quietly phasing out your job, or even your whole department.

It may be hard to tell if your job has been phased out, but there are some telltale signs. If you haven't seen any executives lately your job may have been phased out, but this isn't always a sure sign as they may just be in hiding. If you haven't received any memos or emails about meetings, parties, or betting pools your job may have been phased out.

If you haven't had any coworkers try to borrow money from you or come to think of it if you haven't seen any of your coworkers lately, your job may have been phased out. If you have to go through the window to get into the office because your key no longer fits the locks, your job may have been phased out.

If you are experiencing any of these things your job may have been phased out and the higher-ups just neglected to tell you (which happens more often than you might think). However, if you are still receiving a paycheck it may be a ploy to get you to quit.

Fired. If you are fired it is probably safe to say that your corporate life has not been what you hoped it to be. We can assure you, however, that most of the top executives in the corporate world today have been fired at least once, if not repeatedly. There was a time when firing from the corporation was a much more painful process as employees were literally 'fired.'

Depending on the offense for which a person was dismissed, execution of some form has always been a popular method of getting rid of employees primarily because it reduced retirement pension expenses. Perhaps the most important development in this area was the French corporate use of the guillotine, which led to the institution of 'severance' pay.

The term fired comes from early corporations' use of the firing squad. Military corporations often 'fired' troublesome employees. It took some time to develop firing squad into what we are familiar with today. At first, the firing squad stood in a circle with the fired employee in the center so they could not run away.

This way, no one could miss the target, however, it led to an acute shortage of the firing squad personnel. After trying several different formations such as the square with little success, the current single-line formation was hit upon by an unfortunate accident when all the other firing squad members were shot.

After the abolition of execution, the firing ritual became more symbolic with the corporate employee being hauled out into a hollow square with his coworkers watching. Then his boss or CEO would proceed to cut the buttons off of his corporate uniform and he would be stripped of any corporate logos or other insignia. Now, the more common practice is to simply tell the employee they have two minutes to collect their belongings and get out of the building and never come back.

Quit. If you quit your job, chances are you are happier now than when you were working for your former boss. You have demonstrated the courage to do what countless corporate employees tell themselves they will do every day, but never do.

However, you will no longer have a regular paycheck, retirement plan, health insurance, and a key to the company washroom. Whatever you decide to do next, if you take a new job in another corporation, or simply to get out of the rat race of the corporate world altogether, we wish you well.

Retired. Reaching retirement is the most distinguished and dignified means of leaving a corporation. It represents a lifetime of dedication and service to the corporate world and everything it stands for. Be careful, however, of 'early retirement' programs. Some corporations use this as a ruse to get rid of employees without having to fire them. The general rule is to be suspicious of being offered early retirement after working less than a year.

For those who have truly reached retirement age one can expect a great deal of ceremony surrounding your farewell. While the eastern corporate world holds elderly people in esteem and often keeps them on staff for their wisdom, the western corporate world would just as well pass your office on to someone much younger with 'new ideas,' because they can pay them less. As a result, you will probably not be asked to stay on in any advisory capacity, but instead you will be given a fond farewell and a push out the door.

The celebration of retirement traditionally includes the presentation of a gold watch or some other nominal symbol of your corporation's esteem for you as an individual. Hopefully, you will have an executive in charge of the ceremony who is cognizant of your feelings of both relief and trepidation at having made it through your corporate life and now facing an uncertain future.

A few kind words from an executive will help to smooth the way. The standard, "it's people like you who made this corporation what it is" is always touching. Unfortunately, some of the more cutthroat executives have replaced that phrase with, "it's people like you I stepped on to get to the top."

150

Cleaning out your desk. Once you have been discharged from the corporation you will have to clean out your desk, if you have one. You can use whatever means you wish to carry this out, but we recommend you leave a note and even a present for the next occupant of your desk. Carving your initials and the date into the desktop is a traditional way of marking the passing of an era.

If the circumstances of your departure are, shall we say, not totally amicable, you may want to leave one of the following presents for the next occupant of your desk.
1. Chewing gum stuck to the underside of the desk,
2. Glue spilled in the desk drawers and locks, or
3. Food stuffs like milk or raw fish inadvertently dropped down behind the drawers. (After a few nice warm days people will wonder what the new guy is doing at his desk that smells so bad.)

When you retire official compensation is generally a pension, as well as a token of your corporation's esteem like a gold watch. If you are fired or quit, the best you can hope for is escaping with your personal effects or the clothes on your back. Many hold this as sadly inadequate and as a result have taken to unofficial compensation.

Unofficial compensation is the same no matter what the circumstances of your leaving. Office supplies like paper, staples, and pens (preferably without the company name on them) are the most popular types of unofficial compensation. Other types range from taking important documents to be sold to the highest bidder to taking returnable bottles from the employee lunchroom. Use your own discretion in these instances.

At last the time has come to say your good-byes. Having retired, quit, or fired, you are now fireproof. At last you are free to do, and more importantly, say what you think. You can call your boss out loud what you muttered under your breath for what seemed like an eternity.

You can release the information you helped suppress to the media or to the appropriate law enforcement agencies. You can tell the auditors where to find the slush accounts. You can clear your mind and clear your conscience just as thoroughly as they are making you clear out your desk. Whatever particular secrets you held you can now unburden yourself thereof.

What now? While parting may be such sweet sorrow, it may also be unrestrained joy. Saying hello to anything means you will eventually have to say goodbye. When and how you say goodbye will determine what you do next.

Now that you are no longer a member of the corporate world, have you ever thought about the exciting opportunities in the civil service, military, or academia?

HH
Heather Hill

www.ingramcontent.com/pod-product-compliance
Lightning Source LLC
Chambersburg PA
CBHW031514040426
42445CB00009B/221